THE
RUMI
COLLECTION

AN ANTHOLOGY OF TRANSLATIONS
OF MEVLÂNA JALÂLUDDIN RUMI

✦ ✦ ✦ ✦ ✦

EDITED BY

Kabir Helminski

WITH AN INTRODUCTION BY

Andrew Harvey

SHAMBHALA

Shambhala Publications, Inc.
2129 13th Street
Boulder, Colorado 80302
www.shambhala.com

© 1998 by Kabir Helminski
Published by agreement with Threshold Books
This edition published 2023

Cover art: Katrina Noble
Cover design: Katrina Noble
Interior design: Lora Zorian

9 8 7 6 5 4 3 2 1

Printed in the United States of America

Shambhala Publications makes every effort to print on acid-free,
recycled paper. Shambhala Publications is distributed worldwide
by Penguin Random House, Inc., and its subsidiaries.

The Library of Congress catalogs the previous edition of this book as follows:
Jall al-Din Rumi, Maulana, 1207–1273
[selections. English. 1999]
The Rumi collection: an anthology of translations of Mevlâna Jalâluddin Rumi/
selected and edited by Kabir Helminski.
p. cm.
Includes bibliographical references (p.).
ISBN 978-1-59030-251-4 (hardcover)
ISBN 978-1-64547-165-3 (2023 paperback)
I. Helminski, Kabir, 1947– . II. Title
PK6480.E5H45   1999
891'.5511–dc21   99–32295CIP

The Rumi Collection

Contents

Acknowledgments

I would like to thank the poet John Peck for his thoughtful reading of this material; the poets Andy Gaus, Michael Wolfe, and Richard Wilbur for sharing their love of the craft of poetry so many years ago; Rabia Kathleen Seidel for her part in researching and preparing the manuscript and the accompanying bibliography; Barbara Campman, Nanci Dailey, Gail Peach, and Lora Zorian, among others, careful listeners who followed the unfolding of all this for so many years at Threshold; and my wife, Camille, for her selfless dedication to everything having to do with Mevlâna.

Introduction

Andrew Harvey

Rumi, the greatest mystic poet of Islam and perhaps of the world, was born in Balkh, in what was then known as the province of Khorassan (now Afghanistan), on September 30, 1207. He died in Konya, in southern Turkey, in his sixty-seventh year, on December 17, 1273, leaving behind him, as a testimony to a life lived on the wildest and greatest heights of the spirit, the *Mathnawi*, a mystical epic in six volumes; the *Divan-i-Kabir*, a collection of thirty-five hundred odes and two thousand quatrains; a book of discourses; and several volumes of letters. After his death, his son, Sultan Valad, crystallized his vision and spiritual practices into the structures of the Mevlevi order, which endured persecution and oppression in many eras, to spread Rumi's vision all over the Islamic world.

Now, through the work and pioneering efforts of European and American translators, Rumi's work is as famous in the West as it has been in the East, cherished by seekers on all paths. What Rumi in his life and work combined at the highest level was the philosophical interest of a Plato, the emotional grandeur and vision of a Christ or Buddha, and the extravagant literary gift of a Shakespeare. Rumi could, in fact, be called the Shakespeare of mystics, for, just as Shakespeare explored all the nuances of human character and of the play of Good and Evil, so Rumi, in his astonishingly rich and complex oeuvre, explored all of the aspects of the extreme, gorgeous drama of the soul's journey to God.

Rumi's real name was Jalâluddin. "Rumi" is derived from "Rum," the region of Anatolia, in Turkey, where he eventually settled. His family was a highly distinguished one of jurists and religious scholars who traced their lineage back to to Abu Bakr, one of the companions of the Prophet Muhammad, and the first caliph after Muhammad's death.

His father, Bahaduddin Valad (whom Rumi venerated) was a famous theologian, Sufi master, and visionary, called by his contemporaries "The Sultan of Scholars." What little survives of his writings shows him to have been a passionate and exalted mystic, like his son.

The epoch Rumi was born into was, like ours, one of chaotic violence and turmoil. The Seljuk Empire was menaced from within by political and religious decadence and from without by Christian invaders from the West and the Mongol armies of Genghis Khan from the East. Rumi's life and spirit were seared early on by this turmoil. At the age of twelve, in 1219, he was forced to flee Balkh with his father, who was being attacked by religious enemies and who foresaw the taking of the city by the Mongols, which would occur a year later.

For a decade, Rumi and his family wandered all over Asia Minor and Arabia. They are said to have made the pilgrimage to Mecca and to have stopped on the way at Nishapur, in central Iran, where the young Rumi met the great Persian mystic

Attar, author of *The Conference of the Birds*, who said of him, "This boy will open a gate in the heart of love and throw a flame into the heart of all mystic lovers." Later in his travels, Rumi also went to Damascus, where he met Ibn Arabi, the greatest Sufi philosopher and metaphysician of his age. The legend goes that when Ibn Arabi saw Rumi walking behind his father, he exclaimed, "Glory be to God, an ocean is walking behind a lake."

At eighteen, Rumi married Gavher-Kathoum, the beautiful daughter of Hodja Charifod, a grandee of Samarkand, and fathered two sons with her. After stays in Laranda and Arzanian, in Armenia, Rumi's father was invited, in 1229, by Alaudin Kaykobad, the sultan of Konya in southern Turkey, to go and live there. The sultan built a college for him in Konya, where he taught for two years, until his death in 1231. Immediately afterward, Rumi was chosen to be his successor. Already his brilliance and spiritual depth had made him preeminent in his world. He was only twenty-four years old.

Rumi's first teacher of the path was an old disciple of his father's named Muhaqqiq Tirmidhi. Rumi studied with him for nine years, during which he again went on his travels. After seven years of teaching and studying in Syria, Rumi returned to Konya with a formidable array of spiritual and intellectual skills and became a famous teacher of jurisprudence and canonical law, as well as a spiritual director who soon amassed a vast following. By 1244, wrote his son Sultan Valad in *Secret Word*, Rumi had ten thousand disciples.

For all his achievement, however, Rumi seems to have been inwardly dissatisfied. Sultan Valad tells us that during this period, his father used to pray constantly to meet one of God's hidden saints and be transformed by him. His prayer was to be answered. Toward the end of 1244, probably in late November or early December, Rumi met the man who was to become his soul's beloved and transfigure his life, Shams of Tabriz. Later, Rumi described the meaning of this all-transforming encounter: "I was raw, then I was cooked, then I was ash." In one of his odes, Rumi writes of Shams:

> I have seen the king with a face of Glory,
> He who is the eye and the sun of heaven,
> He who is the companion and healer of all beings,
> He who is the soul and the universe that births souls.

Shams of Tabriz, a strange wild man, a hermit and a wanderer, was in his sixties when he and Rumi met. His ferocious, often scornful temperament had made him many enemies. Legend has it that Shams had prayed for years to meet someone who could stand the grandeur and uncompromising intensity of his presence and receive the full transmission of everything Divine Love had taught him. One day, it is said, God spoke to him and asked him what he would give in exchange. Shams offered Him his life. Then God told him to go to Konya, where he would meet the mystic beloved destined for him, Jalaluddin, the son of Bahaduddin of Balkh.

As to how Rumi and Shams actually encountered each other, no one is really sure. In my opinion, the loveliest of all the many versions is that Shams accosted Rumi as he was riding a donkey through the streets of Konya, followed by a horde of disciples. Shams challenged Rumi: "Who was the greatest of all mystics, Bayazid [a Sufi prophet] or Muhammad?"

"That is a bizarre question, considering that Muhammad was beyond all prophets," Rumi replied. Shams then said, "So what then did Muhammad mean when he told God, 'I didn't know you as I should have,' while Bayazid said, 'Glory be to me, how exalted is my dignity'?"

Rumi answered, "Bayazid's thirst was more easily quenched and the container of his comprehension filled by a single mouthful. The light entered in proportion to the opening of his heart, but the Elect of God, peace and blessings upon him, had a profound desire that needed to be satisfied. For the Prophet, peace and blessings upon him, it was thirst upon thirst; his blessed chest had become God's vast dominion, expanded by the passage from the Qur'an 'Have we not opened up your heart?' [Qur'an 94:1]. So he seemed to be always thirsty. Every day, he came closer to God. For that reason he said: 'I have not known You as I should have.'"

At these words, Shams realized that he had met the one he yearned for, a person capable of receiving what he had to give. Rumi must have also realized that he was face-to-face with the answer to his prayers. At this point, Rumi let out a cry and fainted; he remained unconscious for one hour. When he came to his senses he took Shams's hand and they returned to the college on foot, where they remained in total seclusion for forty days.

Rumi is reported to have said, "When Shams asked me that question, I saw a window open at the top of my head and smoke came out that reached to the Heavenly Throne." Having abandoned teaching and the school, he became absorbed in contemplation of the mysteries of the Soul. A massive transformation of Rumi's heart and whole being now began to take place in a transmission from Shams's heart to his. Shams knew he had very little time and that Rumi had to be utterly remade so that the revelations he was destined to transmit would be potent in him.

Many in Konya became increasingly jealous of Shams's influence on their teacher: Shams was forced to flee Konya and travel to Damascus. Destroyed by grief, Rumi fell sick and asked his son, Sultan Valad, to go to Syria and bring Shams back. Shams returned, but with his return, the jealousy and hatred of the disciples boiled over again and became more menacing. On the evening of December 3, 1244, Shams and Rumi were sitting in Rumi's house. There was a knock at the door. Shams spoke this verse from the Qur'an: "The sun and the moon have their predetermined course which none can deter." Shams rose calmly, went out to the night, and was never seen again. He was almost certainly murdered by a group of disciples, which may have included Rumi's oldest son.

For several years, Rumi continued to hope desperately that Shams was still alive. Twice, in an agony of longing and grief, he went to Damascus to try and find Shams, astounding everyone by the torrent of mystical poetry that now gushed from him. He had been an intellectual and a scholar. Mystic passion and agony now transformed him into a poet.

It was during Rumi's second visit to Damascus that the

ultimate mystery of Shams's and Rumi's mystical love affair started to unfold in him. This is how Sultan Valad, in *Secret Word*, describes what happened to his father in those days: "He didn't see Shams of Tabriz in Syria. He saw him in himself, clear as the moon. He said 'Although I am far from you physically, without body or soul, we are one single light.... I am him, he is me, O seeker.'"

Through loving the eternal beloved in Shams, Rumi had been transformed into love itself: Shams now lived within him. This astounding and healing revelation steadied Rumi. His life grew calmer, and he was able to make the very difficult inner transition from being an agonized and impassioned mystic to becoming one of those rare beings like Jesus or the Buddha whose integral realization continues to haunt and instruct all seekers.

During the next twenty years, Rumi was also to meet two other "heart-friends," in Zarkubi and Husamuddin Chelebi, who would help him deepen his knowledge of divine human love and accompany him on his journey into universal sagedom, which unfolded until and beyond his death.

Now an achieved spiritual master, Rumi went on living in Konya, collecting around him disciples of all kind and classes, writing his mystical masterpiece, the *Mathnawi*, and living a life of awe-inspiring beauty, truth, and humility, which led him to win the tender admiration of all the religious of Konya—Jews and Christians as well as Muslims.

I remember one afternoon in Paris, fifteen years ago, sitting with the great Islamic scholar and translator Eva de Vitray-Meyerovitch, and talking about Rumi. There was a single big red rose open on the table between us, and at a certain moment, the late sun fell on it and seemed to light it up from within. Eva stopped talking, pointed to the rose, and said, "In Rumi, the full rose of the human divine opened. He achieved maturity and greatness in every conceivable way—as a father, as a husband, as a supreme spiritual teacher and inventor of wonderful new spiritual forms and structures, and as the greatest of all mystic poets. He gave a sign to us all forever of what is possible in a life surrendered wholly to the light."

The final teaching of a great spiritual being is in the way he or she dies. Rumi died with a sublime peacefulness and confidence. In the autumnal days of 1273, Rumi started to fade away. Physicians found water in his side, but could not diagnose why he was so weak. When a friend came to visit him in his last illness and was praying for his recovery, Rumi recited:

Why should I be unhappy?
Each parcel of my being is in full bloom.
Why should I not leave this pit?
Haven't I got a solid rope?
I constructed a pigeon house for the pigeons of the soul.
Oh, bird of my soul, fly away now
For I possess a hundred fortified towers.

On December 17, 1273, at sunset, with the sky turning to red flame, as if to welcome him, Rumi died. To this day, Sufis celebrate this date as that of "Shebi-Arus," Rumi's wedding night. Not long before, Rumi had written in a letter to one of his disciples: "When our guides and those who are cherished by us leave and disappear, they are not annihilated, they are like stars that vanish into the light of the sun of reality."

Rumi in English[*]

Kabir Helminski

The phenomenon of Rumi's popularity in America in the last two decades cries for some explanation. As both a translator and publisher in this field, I have observed the interest continually increasing. Not only has his translated work outsold all other poets, it has been read by many people who were not previously interested in either poetry or spiritual writing. His work is being quoted by authors writing not only in traditions other than Sufism—namely, Buddhism, Hinduism, and Christianity—but also in the fields of psychology, health, science, and government.

Somehow, Rumi has given voice to an unconscious yearning in the Western psyche. A Christian minister who was given her first book of Rumi made this comment, "I cannot believe I spent several years in graduate school and I was never given anything like this to read!" A poet wrote to me, "All my years of reading poetry never prepared me for Rumi. I have encountered no writing that affects me so deeply."

What is it that strikes the modern reader in Rumi's words?

[*] A talk given at an international conference on Rumi held at Columbia University in June 1997.

First of all he is perceived as a universal voice calling to us from beyond the concerns of conventional religiosity and limiting beliefs.

There is no doubt that Mevlâna is a universal human being, one who transcended the limitations of his culture and era. In his spiritual attainment he went beyond blind faith to spiritual certainty, but it never weakened his loyalty and love for the Quranic revelation and the Prophetic inheritance. It is very difficult for modern Americans, disillusioned as they are with institutional religion and religious doctrines, to understand how it is possible to reach this state and remain a Muslim. For the Muslim mystic, however, Islam remains an ample field for the liberated mind and heart.

The second reason for his popularity might be that the boundary between Divine and human love is left ambiguous.

Many of the first translations of Mevlâna have been those that could be interpreted as a kind of mystical eroticism. It is not fair to blame the translators for this. Much of Mevlâna's expression during his early, intoxicated period is intensely ecstatic, with a flavor of the erotic:

> I would love to kiss you.
> *The price of kissing is your life.*
> Now my loving is running toward my life shouting,
> *What a bargain, let's buy it.*

Furuzanfar #388

This kind of poetry has caused one magazine of literary erotica to offer a volume of Rumi as a bonus for new subscribers! So

Rumi's appeal is approaching universality. But the trained mystic is sensitive to the relationship between metaphor and reality. For the earthly lover, however, this poetry elevates the sensibilities, spiritualizes the love relationship, and raises it to incandescence. This is not the first time that this kind of influence has entered the Euro-Christian world from Islamic culture. It has its precedent in the period of the Provençal troubadours who transmitted a poetic impulse from Islamic Spain.

Mevlâna not only explicitly addressed the relationship of human and Divine love, he offered a spirituality that was profoundly relational. Not only do all loves lead eventually to the Divine love, but there is a mystery and possibility in spiritual friendship and dialogue. In his relationship with Shams, Husammedin, and Salaheddin, Mevlâna modeled a rare form of relationship: the meeting of two beings who are each reflections of the Divine for each other. Some people see in this a step beyond even the very privileged, yet hierarchical relationship of sheikh and mureed. Perhaps it is the fulfillment of the hadith: "The believer (*mu'min*) is the mirror of the believer (*mu'min*)," a relationship where there is no power or privilege exercised by one over another, or, in other words, a relationship of true love.

Our third point has to do with ecstasy and intoxication. Mevlâna is an ecstatic in a modern world starved for real ecstasy.

There is such a longing in our synthetic and technological culture for something that is natural and ecstatic. Spiritual experience should carry us beyond our mundane concerns to an experience of our essential human nature and our true spiritual home. Alcohol consumption and drug addiction are dim and distorted reflections of this longing of the human soul for freedom and union. But, of course, Sufism is much more than "a body of techniques for producing ecstasy." As we know, particularly from a mature mystic like Shams of Tabriz, there is a sobriety that encompasses intoxication. If anyone will read Shams's *Maqalat*, it is clear that this person who had such an intoxicating effect on Mevlâna was himself rather sober, even if his effect on Rumi was intoxicating.

Finally, what I think is the most significant value of Mevlâna: he is the clearest, most powerful voice of cosmic, Divine love.

He awakens us to the fact that not only is God the Beloved of the human being—which is radical enough in our post-Judeo-Christian culture—but even more shocking and profound, *the human being is the beloved of God.*

If we look up the word "translate" in the dictionary, we find that the origin of its meaning is to move a saint's body or relics from one place to another. The translation of Mevlâna's words is the carrying of that sainthood into our time and culture.

In choosing to translate anything we should ask what was the intention or function of the original work. A work in the field of science calls for a different kind of translation than a work of poetry. The translation of poetry must always be the most subjective form of translation. What I mean by subjective here is the felt presence of an individuality. Not only is an individuality the proximate source of the poetry, but the poetry also must be transmitted through the sensibilities of another poet. Of course, the success of the poetry translated will depend on the degree to which the qualities of the original are preserved and expressed.

In the East, the relationship between master and apprentice dictates that the apprentice's qualities be assimilated to the master's qualities. In the West, a great deal more emphasis is placed on individuality and originality. From the Western translator of Sufi poetry we should expect a little of both: to some extent the translator must allow himself or herself to be annihilated in the presence of the master, and at the same time the living inspiration must find a form with the greatest contemporary poetic potential.

What is it in poetry that causes its effect? How similar are the poetic potentials of one language to another?

In Rumi's case, there is the container of meter and rhyme into which the content of language is poured. In contemporary American poetry, the artifice of rhyme and meter has been somewhat out of favor for most of the last century. The rhythms have shifted from controlled and predictable patterns to patterns that reflect a different sense of improvisation: a phrasing founded on the human breath.

In the domain of meaning, the Persian and Arabic vocabularies seem to offer more levels of meaning than English typically does, so we cannot expect the same kind of allusiveness from English. We must use the levels of meaning available in English. Since there is rarely a correspondence between the levels of meaning in one language and another, if the English is to contain levels of meaning they must be original and yet consistent with the original intent of the poetry.

The choice of what to emulate in the poetry of Rumi must in the end be left up to the skills and inspiration of the translator.

Personally, I would choose to remain fairly close to the original rhythm of the original, and to try to preserve some of its sublime tone. At the same time, since economy is a virtue in poetry, I have often preferred those Anglo-Saxon words that have fewer syllables over those Latinate words that have more syllables:

> Listen to the reed and the tale it tells,
> how it sings of separation.
> Ever since they tore me from the reed bed
> my wail has caused men and women to weep.
> I want a heart torn open with longing
> so that I may relate the pain of this love.

Only the word "separation" has more than one or two syllables, and I was happy to use it because it causes the listener's mind to dwell on the idea itself:

> *How it sings of sep-a-ra-tion . . .*

That one word equals the other four words in the eight-syllable line.

By what criteria may we judge the success of a translation? I would like to offer an example of a successful English translation. Let me point out that I began by choosing one of the most

quoted of the English translations, and then I went back to the
Farsi to see what was there. Here is the English:

> The human shape is a ghost
> made of distraction and pain.
> Sometimes pure light, sometimes cruel,
> trying wildly to open,
> this image tightly held within itself.

Now here is the Farsi:

> een soorate aadamee ke dar ham bastand
> naqsh-i ast ke dar taweelaye gham bastand
> gheh div gahee farishteh ghaahee vehshee
> een khud che talism ast ke muhkam bastand.

Now here is my own translation:

> This human face they fashioned
> is a design in the shape of pain:
> part god, part angel, part savage.
> What a magic charm they've sealed!

This translation takes a fairly rigorous approach to mean-
ing and meter, while using alliteration, as well as levels of mean-
ing in the central word, "charm," which can mean both a magic
talisman and a quality of the heart. It is significantly more ac-
curate, and I think fairly successful, but I would not say that it

is a better poem than the Coleman Barks version, or even that it more successfully communicates the original inspiration. Curious to explore the possibilities, I continued to work with it. Here is another version of mine which I like more:

This human face is a shape
tethered in the stall of pain:
part god, part angel, part beast . . .
a cryptic charm, rarely released.

Some of the best versions can be criticized as translations because they introduce imagery and details that simply do not exist in the original, and yet it is as if their meanings explode from the original text and are completely consistent with it while making use of the possibilities of the American idiom.

The mind of the poet works in this pattern of pain, a place beyond linear logic, a multidimensional world of sound, rhythm, pattern, meaning, and reason all at once. The poet shuffles all of these dimensions until he finds a shape, a structure that begins to hold the meaning and the essence of what is compelling him to communicate.

Let us return once again to this question of what so greatly compelled Rumi to communicate. Why did he write? What was he trying to express?

Every shop has a different kind of merchandise:
the Mathnawi is the workshop for spiritual poverty, O son.
In the shoemaker's shop there is fine leather:

if you see wood there it is only the mold for a shoe.
The drapers have silk and dun-colored cloth in their shops:
if iron is there, it is only to serve as a yardstick.
Our Mathnawi is the shop for Unity:
anything you see there other than the One God
is but an idol.

MATHNAWI VI, 1525–1528

But what is the relationship of this spiritual poverty to this Unity? What are its realities and implications for the human being? It is this, above all, that must somehow be translated. If we lose this, we have lost everything. Such a loss stems from more than linguistic incapacity; it comes from the limits of our sensibility. While we made Rumi popular in the Western world during the late twentieth century, it is also possible that we have re-created him in the likeness of what we can imagine and easily understand: a spiritual rebel, a supremely independent explorer of consciousness, faithful mostly to his own ecstatic vision.

Many writers have related the tale of the first meeting of Rumi with Shams of Tabriz, that mysterious vagabond who set Rumi's soul ablaze. As the tale is most often told,

One day as Shams was seated at the gate of an inn, Jalal came by, riding on a mule, in the midst of a crowd of disciples and students on foot. Shams arose, advanced, and took hold of the mule's bridle, addressing Rumi with these words: "Exchanger of the current coins of deep meaning, who knows the qualities of our Sustainer! Tell me, was Muhammad the greater servant of God or Bayazid Bistami?"

Rumi answered him: "Muhammad was incomparably the greater—the greatest of all prophets and saints."

"Then," responded Shams, "how is it that Muhammad said, 'We have not known Thee as Thou ought to be known,' whereas Bayazid said, 'Glory unto me. How great is my glory'?

On hearing this question, he fainted. On recovering his consciousness, he took his new acquaintance.

Now, who fainted? And this story is mentioned to suggest that Rumi was a somewhat conventional man of religion before his meeting with Shams. And this encounter was supposed to have awakened Rumi to the realization that there is a unitive state beyond orthodox religion with which supposedly the Sufis, but not Muhammad, were acquainted.

Actually, Rumi had already undergone extensive mystical training for years, culminating in three consecutive forty-day fasts in which he lived on only a few crusts of barley bread and some water. He had already been pronounced perfect in his attainment of mystical knowledge.

Well, it turns out there are two versions of this story in the *Menaqib ul-Arifin*, an early Mevlevi text, but only the shorter version, for some reason, has been translated into English in *Legends of the Sufis*, by James Redhouse. The *Menaqib* tells stories about the life of Rumi from different points of view, and a more complete version of the meeting is in the section devoted to Shams! In this longer version, Mevlâna answers Shams with these words:

> "Bayazid's thirst was quenched after one drink, and he boasted of being satiated, and the jar of his comprehension was filled with that portion. The amount of light he received was only as much as would come through the window of his abode.
>
> "As for Muhammad, he kept asking to be given more to drink. His thirst was in his thirst . . . His blessed heart could be described by the words 'have we not expanded for you your heart?' [Qur'an 94:1]. Therefore he would talk of thirst, and every day he grew in asking God to allow him to come closer. Of these two claims, the claim of Mustafa [Muhammad] is greater.
>
> "As for Bayazid, he thought that he was complete when he arrived at God, and did not seek more. But Mustafa, peace be upon him, saw more every day, and went further and further. Day by day, even hour by hour, he would see more and more of the Divine Lights, Majesty, Power, and Wisdom. It was on this account that he said, "We have not known Thee as Thou ought to be known."'
>
> In that moment Shams uttered a cry and fainted.

I would like to end with a ghazal of Mevlâna's that describes the pain of the human being who longs unceasingly for Reality:

Because I cannot sleep
I make music at night.
I am troubled by the one
whose face has the color of spring flowers.
I have neither sleep nor patience,
neither a good reputation nor disgrace.

A thousand robes of wisdom are gone.
All my good manners have moved a thousand miles away.

The heart and the mind are left angry with each other.
The stars and the moon are envious of each other.
Because of this alienation the physical universe
is getting tighter and tighter.

The moon says, "How long will I remain
suspended without a sun?"
Without Love's jewel inside of me,
let the bazaar of my existence be destroyed stone by stone.
O Love, You who have been called by a thousand names,
You who know how to pour the wine
into the chalice of the body,
You who give culture to a thousand cultures,
You who are faceless but have a thousand faces,
O Love, You who shape the faces
of Turks, Europeans, and Zanzibaris,
give me a glass from Your bottle,
or a handful of bheng from Your branch.
Remove the cork once more.

Then we'll see a thousand chiefs prostrate themselves,
and a circle of ecstatic troubadours will play.
Then the addict will be freed of craving.
and will be resurrected,
and stand in awe till Judgment Day.

· 1 ·

Working with Our Humanness

SOMEONE SAID, "There is something I have forgotten." There
is one thing in the world that should not be forgotten. You may
forget everything except that one thing, without there being any
cause for concern. If you remember everything else but forget
that one thing, you will have accomplished nothing. It would
be as if a king sent you to a village on a specific mission. If you
went and performed a hundred other tasks, but neglected to
accomplish the task for which you were sent, it would be as
though you had done nothing. The human being therefore has
come into the world for a specific purpose and aim. If one does
not fulfill that purpose, one has done nothing. *We proposed the
faith unto the heavens, and the earth, and the mountains: and they
refused to undertake it, and were afraid of it; but the human being
undertook it: and yet truly, he was unjust to himself, and foolish.*
[Qur'an 33:72]

FIHI MA FIHI #4*

---

* Fihi ma fihi ["In it what is in it"] contains the discourses of Rumi. It has
been published as *Signs of the Unseen* by Threshold Books. Excerpts ap-
pearing here have been modified stylistically for the purposes of this book.

Your Worth

You know the value of every article of merchandise,
but if you don't know the value of your own soul,
it's all foolishness.
You've come to know the fortunate and the inauspicious stars,
but you don't know whether you yourself
are fortunate or unlucky.
This, this is the essence of all sciences—
that you should know who you will be
when the Day of Reckoning arrives.

MATHNAWI III, 2652–2654
(translated by Kabir Helminski and Camille Helminski)

+ + +

The human shape is a ghost
made of distraction and pain.
Sometimes pure light, sometimes cruel,
trying wildly to open,
this image tightly held within itself.

FURUZANFAR #568
(translated by John Moyne and Coleman Barks)

The Embryo

When the time comes for the embryo
to receive the spirit of life,
at that time the sun begins to help.
This embryo is brought into movement,

for the sun quickens it with spirit.
From the other stars this embryo
received only an impression,
until the sun shone upon it.
How did it become connected
with the shining sun
in the womb?

By ways hidden from our senses:
the way whereby gold is nourished,
the way a common stone becomes a garnet
and the ruby red,
the way fruit is ripened,
and the way courage comes
to one distraught
with fear.

MATHNAWI I, 3775–3782
(translated by Kabir Helminski and Camille Helminski)

BY THE SOUND OF THEIR VOICE

If you hear a secret from a friend at midnight,
you'll know that friend when he speaks to you at dawn;
and if two people bring news to you in the night,
you'll recognize them both in the daylight
by the way they speak.
If during the dark of night the sound of a lion
and the sound of a dog

enter someone's ear
and he could not see them in the dark,
when day breaks and they begin to speak again,
the intelligent hearer will know them by their voice.
And so it is, that both the Devil and the angelic Spirit
present us with objects of deisre
to awaken our power of choice.
There is an invisible strength within us;
when it recognizes two opposing objects of desire,
it grows stronger.

MATHNAWI V, 3000–3005
(translated by Kabir Helminski and Camille Helminski)

✦ ✦ ✦

The love of women
is made attractive to men.
God has arranged it: how can they avoid
what God has arranged?
Inasmuch as God created woman
so that Adam might take comfort in her,
how can Adam be parted from Eve?
Woman is a ray of God.
She is not that earthly beloved:
she is creative, not created.

MATHNAWI I, 2435–2437
(translated by Kabir Helminski and Camille Helminski)

Everything that is made beautiful and fair and lovely
is made for the eye of one who sees.

MATHNAWI I, 2383
(translated by Kabir Helminski and Camille Helminski)

+ + +

If love were only spiritual,
the practices of fasting and prayer would not exist.
The gifts of lovers to one another are,
in respect to love, nothing but forms;
yet, they testify
to invisible love.

MATHNAWI I, 2625–2627
(translated by Kabir Helminski and Camille Helminski)

THIS MARRIAGE

May these vows and this marriage be blessed.
May it be sweet milk,
this marriage, like wine and halvah.
May this marriage offer fruit and shade
like the date palm.
May this marriage be full of laughter,
our every day a day in paradise.
May this marriage be a sign of compassion,
a seal of happiness here and hereafter.
May this marriage have a fair face and a good name,
an omen as welcome

as the moon in a clear blue sky.
I am out of words to describe
how spirit mingles in this marriage.

FURUZANFAR #2667
(translated by Kabir Helminski)

THERE'S NOTHING AHEAD

Lovers think they're looking for each other,
but there's only one search: wandering
this world is wandering that, both inside one
transparent sky. In here
there is no dogma and no heresy.

The miracle of Jesus is himself, not what he said or did
about the future. Forget the future.
I'd worship someone who could do that!

On the way you may want to look back, or not,
but if you can say, There's nothing ahead,
there will be nothing there.

Stretch your arms and take hold the cloth of your clothes
with both hands. The cure for pain is in the pain.
Good and bad are mixed. If you don't have both,
you don't belong with us.
When one of us gets lost, is not here, he must be inside us.
There's no place like that anywhere in the world.

FURUZANFAR #425
(translated by John Moyne and Coleman Barks)

Those You Are With

What is a real connection between people? When the same
    knowledge
opens a door between them. When the same inner sight exists
in you as in another, you are drawn to be companions.
When a man feels in himself the innermost nature of a woman,
he is drawn to her sexually. When a woman
feels the masculine self of a man within her,
she wants him physically in her.

When you feel the qualities of Gabriel in you, you fly up quickly
like a fledgling not thinking of the ground.
When you feel asinine qualities in you, no matter how you try
to do otherwise, you will head toward the stable.
The mouse is not despicable for its form, which is a helpless victim
to birds of prey, the mouse who loves dark places and cheese
and pistachio nuts and syrup. When the white falcon, though,
has the inner nature of a mouse, it is a disgrace to all animals.
    Angelic figures and criminals
shackled head-down in a pit are similar looking,
same arms, same head. Moses is a bright spirit.
Pharaoh disgusting with his sorcery.

Always search for your innermost nature in those you are with.
As rose oil imbibes from roses.
Even on the grave of a holy man, a holy man lays his face
and hands and takes in light.

MATHNAWI VI, 2992–3008
(*translated by Coleman Barks*)

Traveling Companions

The one who cheerfully goes alone on a journey—
if he travels with companions
his progress is increased a hundredfold.
Notwithstanding the insensitivity of a donkey,
even the donkey is exhilarated, O dervish,
by comrades of its own kind
and so becomes capable of exerting strength.

To a donkey who goes alone and away from the caravan,
the road is made longer a hundredfold by fatigue.
How much more it suffers the crop and the whip
that it might cross the desert by itself!
That ass is implicitly telling you, "Pay attention!
Don't travel alone like this, unless you are an ass!"
Beyond a doubt the one
who cheerfully goes alone into the toll house
proceeds more cheerfully with companions.
Every prophet on this straight path
produced the testimony of miracles and sought fellow
    travelers.

MATHNAWI VI, 512–518
(translated by Kabir Helminski and Camille Helminski)

Praising Manners

We should ask God
to help us toward manners. Inner gifts
do not find their way
to creatures without just respect.

If a man or woman flails about, he not only
smashes his house,
he burns the world down.

Your depression is connected to your insolence
and refusal to praise. Whoever feels himself walking
on the path, and refuses to praise—that man or woman
steals from others every day—is a shoplifter!

The sun became full of light when it got hold of itself.
Angels only began shining when they achieved discipline.
The sun goes out whenever the cloud of not-praising comes.
The moment the foolish angel felt insolent, he heard the
    door close.

(translated by Robert Bly)

The Ears

The big ear on the outside of our head could be closed.
It is so good at hearing that the inner ear goes deaf.
What if you had no hearing at all, no nose, no mind-stuff!
Then one could hear well the three syllables: "Turn around."

Our sounds, our work, our renown, these are outer.
When we move inwardly, we move through inner space.
Our feet walk firmly, they experience sidewalks well.
There is one inside who walks like Jesus on the sea.

(translated by Robert Bly)

The Jar with the Dry Rim

The mind is an ocean ... I and so many worlds
are rolling there, mysterious, dimly seen!
And our bodies? Our body is a cup, floating
on the ocean; soon it will fill, and sink....
Not even one bubble will show where it went down.
The spirit is so near that you can't see it!
But reach for it ... don't be a jar
full of water, whose rim is always dry.
Don't be the rider who gallops all night
and never sees the horse that is beneath him.

(translated by Robert Bly)

The Mill, the Stone, and the Water

All our desire is a grain of wheat.
Our whole personality is the milling-building.
But this mill grinds without knowing about it.

The millstone is your heavy body.
What makes the stone turn is your thought-river.
The stone says: I don't know why we do all this, but the river
    has knowledge!

If you ask the river, it says,
I don't know why I flow.
All I know is that a human opened the gate!
And if you ask the person, he says:

All I know, oh gobbler of bread, is that if this stone
stops going around, there'll be no bread for your bread-soup!
All this grinding goes on, and no one has any knowledge!
So just be quiet, and one day turn
to God, and say: "What is this about bread-making?"

(translated by Robert Bly)

What Is This Fragrance?

what is this fragrance?
is it from heaven?
whose laughter is this?
is it Houris in paradise?

what wedding is this
with moon for a platter
and heaven for a veil?

what banquet is this
that the Sultan of Baghdad
licks the platters
in our kitchen?

God alone knows!
but come! Take a pick-axe
and break apart
your stony self

the heart's matrix
is glutted with rubies
springs of laughter
are buried in your breast

unstop the wine jar,
batter down the door
to the treasury of nonexistence

the water in your jug
is brackish and low

smash the jug
and come to the river!

(translated by Daniel Liebert)

INWARD OCCUPATION

When Satan sees, to the left or right, anyone who is perfect,
he becomes ill with envy,
for every wretch whose stack has been burnt
is unwilling that anyone else's candle should be lighted.
Pay attention and work on perfecting yourself,
so that the perfection of others may not grieve you.
Beg of God the removal of envy,
that God may deliver you from externals,
and bestow upon you an inward occupation,
which will absorb you
so that your attention is not drawn away.

MATHNAWI IV, 2678–2682
(translated by Kabir Helminski and Camille Helminski)

+ + +

Make real the sublime words of the Prophet:
"We are the last and the foremost."
The fresh and perfect fruit is the last thing to come into existence
For although the fruit is the last thing to come into existence,
It is, in fact, the first, for it was the goal.

(translated by Andrew Harvey)

ANSWERS FROM THE ELEMENTS

A whole afternoon field inside me from one stem of reed.
The messenger comes running toward me, irritated:
Why be so hard to find?

Last night I asked the moon about the Moon, my one question
for the visible world, Where is God?
The moon says, *I am dust stirred up*
when he passed by. The sun, *My face is pale yellow*
from just now seeing him. Water: *I slide on my head and face*
like a snake, from a spell he said. Fire: *His lightning,*
I want to be that restless. Wine, why so light?
I would burn if I had a choice. Earth, quiet
and thoughtful? *Inside me I have a garden*
and an underground spring.

This world hurts my head with its answers,
wine filling my hand, not my glass.
If I could wake completely, I would say without speaking
why I'm ashamed of using words.

FURUZANFAR #1692
(translated by Coleman Barks)

· 2 ·

The Ego Animal

THERE ARE THREE KINDS OF BEINGS. The first are the angels, who are pure intelligence. It is their nature and means of sustenance to be obedient, worshipful, and constantly mindful. That is what they feed on and live by, like a fish in water, whose life is of the water and whose bed and pillow are the water. Angels are not obliged to do what they do. Since they are abstract and free from lust, what favor do they incur for not being lustful or not having carnal desires? Being pure, they do not have to struggle against conceiving passions. If they perform acts of obedience, they are not counted as such because such is their nature and they cannot be otherwise.

The second kind are the animals, who are pure instinct and have no conscious will. They are also under no moral obligation like poor man, who is a mixture of intelligence and lust. Half of him is angelic and half animal. Half serpent and half fish, his fish pulls him toward the water and his serpent toward the dust. They are in a constant tug-of-war. "He whose intellect overcomes his lust is higher than the angels; he whose lust overcomes his intelligence is less than an animal."

The angel is free because of his knowledge,
the beast because of his ignorance.
Between the two remains the son of man to struggle.*

Fihi ma Fihi #17

Wings of Desire

People are distracted by objects of desire,
and afterward repent of the lust they've indulged,
because they have indulged with a phantom
and are left even farther from Reality than before.
Your desire for the illusory could be a wing,
by means of which a seeker might ascend to Reality.
When you have indulged a lust, your wing drops off;
you become lame, abandoned by a fantasy.
Preserve the wing and don't indulge such lust,
so that the wing of desire may bear you to Paradise.
People fancy they are enjoying themselves,
but they are really tearing out their wings
for the sake of an illusion.

Mathnawi III, 2133–2138
(translated by Kabir Helminski and Camille Helminski)

* The line occurs in Rumi, Divan, II, ghazal 918, line 9669.

SELECTIONS FROM THE MATHNAWI
(*translated by Kabir Helminski and Camille Helminski*)

The undisciplined man doesn't wrong himself alone—
he sets fire to the whole world.
Discipline enabled Heaven to be filled with light;
discipline enabled the angels to be immaculate and holy.

MATHNAWI I, 79, 91

✦ ✦ ✦

Refresh your faith, but not with talking.
You have secretly refreshed your desires.
As long as desires are fresh, faith is not,
for it is these desires that lock that gate.

MATHNAWI I, 1078–1079

✦ ✦ ✦

Many of the faults you see in others, dear reader,
are your own nature reflected in them.
As the Prophet said,
"The faithful are mirrors to one another."

MATHNAWI I, 1319, 1328

✦ ✦ ✦

With will, fire becomes sweet water;
and without will, even water becomes fire.

MATHNAWI I, 1336

* * *

O tongue, you are an endless treasure.
O tongue, you are also an endless disease.

MATHNAWI I, 1702

* * *

The world's flattery and hypocrisy is a sweet morsel:
eat less of it, for it is full of fire.
Its fire is hidden while its taste is manifest,
but its smoke becomes visible in the end.

MATHNAWI I, 1855–1856

* * *

Your thinking is like a camel driver,
and you are the camel:
it drives you in every direction under its bitter control.

MATHNAWI I, 2497

* * *

Hungry, you're a dog, angry and bad-natured.
Having eaten your fill, you become a carcass;
you lie down like a wall, senseless.
At one time a dog, at another time a carcass,
how will you run with lions, or follow the saints?

MATHNAWI I, 2873–2875

＊ ＊ ＊

If you are irritated by every rub,
how will your mirror be polished?

MATHNAWI I, 2980

＊ ＊ ＊

I'm the devoted slave
of anyone who doesn't claim
to have attained dining with God
at every way station.
Many inns must be left behind
before you reach your home.

MATHNAWI I, 3259–3261

＊ ＊ ＊

A conceited person sees some sin,
and the flames of Hell rise up in him.
He calls that hellish pride defense of the Religion;
he doesn't notice his own arrogant soul.

MATHNAWI I, 3347–3348

＋ ＋ ＋

Fiery lust is not diminished by indulging it,
but inevitably by leaving it ungratified.
As long as you are laying logs on the fire,
the fire will burn.
When you withhold the wood, the fire dies,
and God carries the water.

Mathnawi I, 3703–3706

· 3 ·

Awe, Naked Wonder

Go and contemplate God's wonders, become lost to yourselves from the majesty and awe of God. When the one who beholds the wonders of God abandons pride and egoism from contemplating God's work, that one will know his proper station and will be silent concerning the Maker. Such a person will only say from their soul, "I cannot praise You properly," because that declaration is beyond reckoning.

Mathnawi IV, 3708–3710

With God there is no room for two egos. You say "I," and He says "I." In order for this duality to disappear, either you must die for Him or He for you. It is not possible, however, for Him to die—either phenomenally or conceptually—because "He is the Ever-living who dieth not." He is so gracious, however, that if it were possible He would die for you in order that the duality might disappear. Since it is not possible for Him to die, you must die so that He may be manifested to you, thus eliminating the duality.

Fihi ma Fihi #24

GIVE ME ECSTASY

Give me ecstasy, give me naked wonder, O my Creator!
Give birth to the Beloved in me, and let this Lover die!
Let a thousand wrangling desires become one Love!
This ring of desire I wear is the seal of Solomon.
I know I have it only on loan, so I never take it off.
The years of repentance are over, a new year has come
That shatters and destroys a thousand regrets a day!
If you never knew this vertigo, this mad Spring will make you
    totter!
O Love, You are the universal soul, crown, and jail all at once;
At once the Prophet's call and our lack of belief.
Love, You have created us with thirsty hearts,
You have bound us to the Source of Splendor.
For You my thorns have blossomed, my atoms embraced the
    worlds.
Contemplating in my leaping atoms the universe
Makes my days stagger and sob with wonder!
Look, the wine is in the green grape, existence in nothingness!
Joseph, I beg you, see in your pit the crown and the kingdom!
A thorn that has not blossomed cannot illumine the field;
How can a being made of water and clay find life
If Divine Breath does not Itself kindle it?
Clap your hands, clap your hands again, and know each sound
Has its origin in the Wine's own self-surrender!
Be silent! Spring is here! The rose is dancing with its thorn.
Beauties have come from the Invisible to call you home.

(translated by Andrew Harvey)

Don't Say Yes or No

The fire of hell is just an atom of God's wrath
Just a whip He wields to menace the evil.
Yes, God's wrath is fiery, all-powerful, all-devouring,
But the freshness of His mercy transcends it.
This is an unconditional, unqualified, spiritual priority.
Have you seen beyond duality what is before and behind?
How could a clay bird soar into the heaven of vision?
The highest place it can soar to is still only air,
For its origin remains sensuality and desire.
Stay, then, astounded and bewildered; don't say "yes" or "no."
Then Mercy can stretch out Its hands to help you.
How could you begin to understand His miracles?
If you said "yes" glibly you would be lying.
And if you say "no," that "no" will behead you
And force severity to slam shut your soul's window.
So stay in bewilderment, in wonder, so God's succor
Can run to you from every side and direction.
When you are really bewildered, maddened, and annihilated,
Then your whole being prays, without words, "Guide me!"
The wrath of God is terrible, more terrible than anything,
But once you have begun to tremble, it starts to soften.
Anger is aimed at the denier; when you have become humble
You will come to know it as gentleness, as mercy.

(translated by Andrew Harvey)

Your Soul Is So Close to Mine

Your soul is so close to mine
I know what you dream.
Friends scan each other's depths;
Would I be a Friend, if I didn't?
A Friend is a mirror of clear water;
I see my gains in you, and my losses.
Turn away from me for one moment
My mouth fills and chokes with gall.
Like a dream that flows from heart to heart,
I, too, flow continually through all hearts.
Everything you think, I know;
Your heart is so close to mine.
I have other symbols, even more intimate,
Come closer still, dare to invoke them.
Come, like a real dervish, and dance among us,
Don't joke, don't boast I am already present.
In the center of your house I am like a pillar,
On your rooftop I bow my head like a gutter.
I turn like a cup in the heart of your assembly;
In the thick of your battles, I strike like an arrow.
When I give my life for yours, what Grace descends!
Each life I give gives you a thousand new worlds!
In this house, there are thousands of corpses.
You sit and say: "Here is my kingdom."
A handful of dust moans: "I was hair."
Another handful whispers: "I was bones."
Another cries: "I was old."

Yet another: "I was young."
Another shouts: "Stop where you are! Stop!
Don't you know who I am! I am so-and-so's son!"
You sit destroyed, astounded, and then suddenly Love
    appears.
"Come closer still," Love says, "it is I, Eternal Life."

(translated by Andrew Harvey)

The Drunkards and the Tavern

I'm drunk and you're insane, who's going to lead us home?
How many times did they say,
"Drink just a little, only two or three at most?"

In this city no one I see is conscious;
one is worse off than the next, frenzied and insane.

Dear one, come to the tavern of ruin
and experience the pleasures of the soul.
What happiness can there be apart
from this intimate conversation
with the Beloved, the Soul of souls?

In every corner there are drunkards, arm in arm,
while the Server pours the wine
from a royal decanter to every particle of being.

You belong to the tavern: your income is wine,
and wine is all you ever buy.
Don't give even a second away
to the concerns of the merely sober.

O lute player, are you more drunk, or am I?
In the presence of one as drunk as you, my magic is a myth.

When I went outside the house,
some drunk approached me,
and in his eyes I saw
hundreds of hidden gardens and sanctuaries.

Like a ship without an anchor,
he rocked this way and that.

Hundreds of intellectuals and wise men
could die from a taste of his yearning.

I asked, "Where are you from?"
He laughed and said, "O soul,
half of me is from Turkestan and half from Farghana.

Half of me is water and mud, half heart and soul;
half of me is the ocean's shore, half is all pearl."

"Be my friend," I pleaded. "I'm one of your family."
"I know the difference between family and outsiders."

I've neither a heart nor a turban,
and here in this house of hangovers
my breast is filled with unspoken words.
Shall I try to explain or not?

Have I lived among the lame for so long
that I've begun to limp myself?
And yet no slap of pain could disturb
a drunkenness like this.

Listen, can you hear a wail
arising from the pillar of grief?
Shams al-Haqq of Tabriz, where are you now,
after all the mischief you've stirred in our hearts?

(translated by K. Helminski, A. Godlas, and L. Saedian)

THE SPIRITUAL CONCERT

Music: the tranquility of life's spirit: but known only to those
     who know life's spirit's spirit
Fall asleep in a garden & you gain by waking—drowse in a
     prison & your waking will be but loss
Make music at weddings not wakes: at times of rejoicing not
     places of lamentation
One blind to his own inner jewel—one from whose eyes that
     moon is hidden—
how could he be worthy of whirling dance & tambourine?
of music which unites us with the Thief of Hearts?
Turn your face toward Mecca, yes, but know this: music is this
     world, music is the other world
and of all the world the circle-dancers turn and turn around
     the pivot of the Kaaba.
You want the Big Rock Candy Mountain? By all means go! a
     single candy cane? Well, that you can have for free.

(translated by Peter Lamborn Wilson)

On His Sepulchre

If wheat grows on my grave, cut it & bake it—the bread will
    make you drunk;
the dough & the baker himself will go mad & the oven fall to
    singing tavern ditties.
If you make a pilgrimage to my grave you'll see my tombstone
    dancing by itself;
don't come without a tambourine—God's holidays should not
    be marred with gloom.
Jaws clamped, sleeping in the grave, the mouth nibbles the
    beloved's opium and sweets;
from every direction trumpets of war & drunkard's harps:
    action begets action, & so forth & so on.
God moulded me from the wine lees of Love—now death has
    effaced me I am Love itself;
I am drunkenness, my root is the wine of love—tell me, what
    comes of wine but intoxication?
It will not stay an instant: my spirit flies to the tower of the
    love of Shamsoddin of Tabriz.

(translated by Peter Lamborn Wilson)

Proper Vocation

Nothing occupies us, Sir,
save service to that cupbearer;
Saki! Another round, please—
& deliver us from Good & Evil.
God, Sir, has created no one
without a proper vocation;
as for us, He has appointed the job
of permanent unemployment:
by day dancing in the light
like motes of dust;
by night, like stars, circumambulating
the moon-visaged beloved.
If He wanted us to work, after all,
He would not have created this wine;
with a skin-full of this, Sir,
would you rush out to commit economics?
What job could a drunkard do
other than the work of the wine itself?
That sacred vintage, transported across
earth & heaven to the Everlasting Refuge.
Drink mere worldly wine, sleep
one night & it passes;
drink from the flagon of the One & your head
will follow you to the grave.
The source of all mercy, Sir,
pours it out for free;
& these sakis treat us as sweetly

as nursemaids their children.
Drink, my heart, & go drunk,
wherever you go, go drunk,
introduce others to this pleasure
& God will keep you well supplied.
Where you witness some beauty
sit & be a mirror;
where you see ugliness
slip the looking glass back in its bag.
Wander happily about the streets
mingling with the young &
beautiful
reciting, "Nay, I swear
by this city . . ."*
bravo!
. . . ah, but my head,
my head is spinning from this wine;
I will dry up & be silent,
I will not sit here & count blessings
which mathematics cannot
comprehend.

(translated by Peter Lamborn Wilson)

---

* Qur'an 90:1. The reference here is to Mecca as the City of Revelation. Rumi intends by extension any city or place wherein beauty and intoxication attain the power of revelation.

The Only Teaching

For lovers, the only teaching is the beauty of the Beloved:
their only book and lecture is the Face.
Outwardly they are silent,
but their penetrating remembrance rises
to the high throne of their Friend.
Their only lesson is enthusiasm, whirling, and trembling,
not the minor details of law.

MATHNAWI III, 3847–3819
(translated by Kabir Helminski and Camille Helminski)

Can Anyone Really Describe

Can anyone really describe the actions of the Matchless One?
Anything I can say is only what I'm allowed to.
Sometimes He acts this way, sometimes in its exact opposite;
The real work of religion is permanent astonishment.
By that I don't mean in astonishment turning your back on
    Him—
I mean: blazing in blind ecstasy, drowned in God and drunk
    on Love.

(translated by Andrew Harvey)

· 4 ·

The Inner Work

SOMEONE SAID, "Mention us in your intention. The intention is the main thing. If there are no words, never mind. Words are secondary." Does this man think that after all, the intention existed in the world of spirits before the world of bodies and that therefore we were brought into the world of bodies to no good purpose? This is absurd, for words are useful and beneficial. If you plant only the kernel of an apricot pit, it will not grow; but if you plant it together with its shell, it will grow. Therefore, we realize that external form is important too. Prayer is internal: "There is no prayer without the presence of the heart," as the Prophet said. However, you must necessarily perform it in external form, with physical bendings and prostrations. Only then do you gain full benefit and reach the goal. *Those . . . who persevere in their prayers* [Qur'an 70:23]. This is the prayer of the spirit. Prayer of the external form is temporary; it is not everlasting because the spirit of this world is an endless ocean. The body is the shore and dry land, which is limited and finite. Therefore, everlasting prayer belongs only to the spirit. The spirit does indeed have a type of bow and prostration; however, bowing and prostrating must be manifested in external form because there is a connection between substance and form. So long as the two do not coincide, there is no benefit. As for your

claim that form is secondary to substance, that form is the sub-
ject, and the heart is king; these are relative terms.

Fihi ma Fihi #38

Why Organize a Universe This Way?

What does not exist looks so handsome.
What does exist, where is it?
An ocean is hidden. All we see is foam,
shapes of dust, spinning, tall as minarets, but I want wind.
Dust can't rise up without wind, I know, but can't I
    understand this
by some way other than induction?

Invisible ocean, wind. Visible foam and dust: this is speech.
Why can't we hear *thought?*
These eyes were born asleep.
Why organize a universe this way?

With the merchant close by a magician measures out
five hundred ells of linen moonlight.
It takes all his money, but the merchant buys the lot.
Suddenly there's no linen, and of course there's no money,
which was his life spent wrongly, and yours.
Say, Save me, Thou One, from witches who tie knots
and blow on them. They're tying them again.
Prayers are not enough. You must do something.

Three companions for you: number one,
what you own. He won't even leave the house
for some danger you might be in. He stays inside.
Number two, your good friend. He at least comes to the funeral.
He stands and talks at the gravesite. No further.

The third companion, what you do, your work,
goes down into death to be there with you,
to help. Take deep refuge
with that companion, beforehand.

MATHNAWI V, 1026–1050
(*translated by Coleman Barks*)

What Have You Bought with Your Life?

On Resurrection Day God will ask,
"During this sojourn I gave you,
what have you produced for Me?
Through what work have you reached your life's end?
For what have your food and your strength been consumed?
Where have you dimmed the luster of your eye?
Where have you dissipated your five senses?
You have expended eyes and ears and intellect
and the pure celestial substances;
what have you purchased from the earth?
I gave you hands and feet as spade and mattock
for tilling the soil of good works;
when did they begin to work by themselves?"

MATHNAWI III, 2149–2153
(*translated by Kabir Helminski and Camille Helminski*)

Ask the Rose about the Rose

The interpretation of a sacred text is true
if it stirs you to hope, activity, and awe;
and if it makes you slacken your service,
know the real truth to be this:
it's a distortion of the sense of the saying,
not a true interpretation.
This saying has come down
to inspire you to serve—
that God may take the hands
of those who have lost hope.
Ask the meaning of the Qur'an from the Qur'an alone,
and from that one who has set fire
to his idle fancy and burned it away,
and has become a sacrifice to the Qur'an,
bowing low in humbleness,
so that the Qur'an has become the essence of his spirit.
If an essential oil that has utterly devoted itself to the rose,
you can smell either that oil or the rose, as you please.

MATHNAWI V, 3125–3130
(*translated by Kabir Helminski and Camille Helminski*)

The Torrent Leaves

Rise up nimbly and go on your strange journey
to the ocean of meanings where you become one of those.
From one terrace to another through clay banks,
washing your wings with watery silt,

follow your friends. The pitcher breaks.
You're in the moving river. Living Water,
how long will you make clay pitchers
that have to be broken to enter you?
The torrent knows it can't stay on this mountain.
Leave and don't look away from the Sun as you go.
Through him you are sometimes crescent, sometimes full.

OPEN SECRET P. 68; FURUZANFAR #2873
(translated by Coleman Barks)

WHEN THINGS ARE HEARD

The ear participates and helps arrange marriages;
the eye has already made love with what it sees.

The eye knows pleasure, delights in the body's shape:
the ear hears words that talk about all this.

When hearing takes place, character areas change;
but when you see, inner areas change.

If all you know about fire is what you have heard
see if the fire will agree to cook you!

Certain energies come only when you burn.
If you long for belief, sit down in the fire!

When the ear receives subtly, it turns into an eye.
But if words do not reach the ear in the chest, nothing
   happens.

(translated by Robert Bly)

Search the Darkness

Sit with your friends; don't go back to sleep.
Don't sink like a fish to the bottom of the sea.

Surge like an ocean,
don't scatter yourself like a storm.

Life's waters flow from darkness.
Search the darkness, don't run from it.

Night travelers are full of light,
and you are, too; don't leave this companionship.

Be a wakeful candle in a golden dish,
don't slip into the dirt like quicksilver.

The moon appears for night travelers,
be watchful when the moon is full.

Furuzanfar #2232
(translated by Kabir Helminski)

The Inner Garment of Love

A soul which is not clothed
with the inner garment of Love
should be ashamed of its existence.

Be drunk with Love,
for Love is all that exists.
Where is intimacy found
if not in the give and take of Love?

If they ask what Love is,
say: the sacrifice of will.
If you have not left your will behind,
you have no will at all.

The lover is a king of kings
with both worlds beneath him;
and a king does not regard
what lies at his feet.

Only Love and the lover
can resurrect beyond time.
Give your heart to this;
the rest is secondhand.

How long will you embrace
a lifeless beloved?
Embrace that entity
to which nothing can cling.

What sprouts up every spring
will wither by autumn,
but the rose garden of Love
is always green.

Both the rose and the thorn
appear together in spring,
and the wine of the grape
is not without its headaches.

Don't be an impatient
bystander on this path—
by God there's no death
worse than expectation.

Set your heart on hard cash
if you are not counterfeit,
and listen to this advice
if you are not a slave:

Don't falter on the horse
of the body; go more lightly on foot.
God gives wings to those
who are not content to ride an ass.

Let go of your worries
and be completely clear-hearted,
like the face of a mirror
that contains no images.

When it is empty of forms,
all forms are contained in it.
No face would be ashamed
to be so clear.

If you want a clear mirror,
behold yourself
and see the shameless truth
which the mirror reflects.

If metal can be polished
to a mirrorlike finish,
what polishing might the mirror
of the heart require?

Between the mirror and the heart
is this single difference:
the heart conceals secrets,
while the mirror does not.

(translated by Kabir Helminski)

· 5 ·

The Step into Placelessness

SOMEONE ASKED, "Is there any way to approach God other than prayer?" The answer is more prayer. However, prayer does not exist only in outward form: that is just the "shell" of prayer because it has a beginning and an end. Anything that has a beginning and an end is a "shell." The proclamation of God's greatness, *Allahu Akbar*, is the beginning of the prayer and the greeting of peace is its end. Likewise, there is more to the pronouncement of faith than what is said with the tongue because it too has a beginning and an end. Anything that can be vocalized and has a beginning and an end is a "form," a "shell"; its "soul," however, is unqualifiable and infinite, without beginning and without end. Anyway, prayer as we know it was formulated by the prophets. Now the Prophet, who formalized our prayer, says, "I have a 'time' with God which neither any prophet who brought a revelation nor any angel intimate with God can share with me." We know then that the "soul" of prayer is not only its external form, but also a state of total absorption and unconsciousness during which all these external forms, for which there is no room, remain outside. In that state there is not even room for a Gabriel, who is but an imaginal form.

FIHI MA FIHI #3

43

To Take a Step without Feet

This is love: to fly toward a secret sky,
to cause a hundred veils to fall each moment
First, to let go of life.
In the end, to take a step without feet.
To regard this world as invisible,
and to disregard what appears to the self.

Heart, I said, what a gift it has been
to enter this circle of lovers,
to see beyond seeing itself,
to reach and feel within the breast.

My soul, where does this breathing arise?
How does this beating heart exist?
Bird of the soul, speak in your own words,
and I will understand.

The heart replied: I was in the workplace
the day this house of water and clay was fired.
I was already fleeing that created house,
even as it was being created.
When I could no longer resist, I was dragged down,
and my features were molded from a handful of earth.

(translated by Kabir Helminski)

Mistaking the Lightning for the Sun

By love what is bitter becomes sweet,
bits of copper turn to gold.
By love the dregs are made clear,
and pain begins to heal.
By love the dead come alive,
and a king becomes a slave.
This love, moreover, is the fruit of knowledge;
no fool will ever sit on the throne of love.
When did a lack of knowledge
ever give birth to this love?
No, ignorance only falls in love
with what is lifeless.
It thinks it sees in something lifeless
the appearance of the one it desires,
as if it heard the beloved whistle.
A lack of knowledge cannot discern;
it mistakes a flash of lightning for the sun.
Lightning is transient and faithless;
without clearness you will not know
the transient from the permanent.
Why is lightning said to laugh?
It is laughing at whoever
sets his heart upon its light.
The lights of the sky are feeble;
they are not like that light which is neither
of the East nor the West.

Regard that lightning as something which
taketh away the sight,
and regard the eternal light as a Helper.
To ride your horse on the foam of the sea,
to read your letter by the flash of lightning
is to fail, because of desire,
to see the end result.
It is to laugh
at your own mind and intelligence.
Intelligence, by its nature, sees the end;
it is your animal side that cannot see the end.
Intelligence overwhelmed by the flesh
becomes flesh; Jupiter checkmated by Saturn
turns inauspicious.
Yet turn your gaze toward this bad luck,
and see the One that brought it to you.
Whoever witnesses this ebb and flow
penetrates from bad luck to good.
God continually turns you
from one state of feeling to another,
revealing truth by means of opposites. . . .
So that you may have
the two wings of fear and hope;
for the bird with one wing is unable to fly. . . .
This bodily world is deceptive,
except for one who has escaped desire.

MATHNAWI II, 1529–1535; 1542–1552; 1554; 1560
(translated by Kabir Helminski)

At the Time of the Night Prayer

At the time of night prayer, as the sun slides down,
the route the senses walk on closes, the route to the invisible
    opens.

The angel of sleep then gathers and drives along the spirits;
just as the mountain keeper gathers his sheep on a slope.

And what amazing sights he offers to the descending sheep!
Cities with sparkling streets, hyacinth gardens, emerald
    pastures.

The spirit sees astounding beings, turtles turned to men,
men turned to angels, when sleep erases the banal.

I think one could say the spirit goes back to its old home;
it no longer remembers where it lives, and loses its fatigue.

It carries around in life so many griefs and loads
and trembles under their weight; they are going, it is all well.

(translated by Robert Bly)

Eating Poetry

My poems resemble the bread of Egypt—one night
passes over it, and you can't eat it anymore.

So gobble them down now, while they're still fresh,
before the dust of the world settles on them.

Where a poem belongs is here, in the warmth of the chest;
out in the world it dies of cold.

You've seen a fish—put him on dry land,
he quivers for a few minutes, and then is still.

And even if you eat my poems while they're still fresh,
you still have to bring forward many images yourself.

Actually, friend, what you're eating is your own imagination.
These are not just a bunch of old proverbs.

(translated by Robert Bly)

SUBTLE DEGREES

subtle degrees
of domination and servitude
are what you know as love

but love is different
it arrives complete
just there
like the moon in the window

like the sun
of neither east nor west
nor of anyplace

when that sun arrives
east and west arrive

desire only that
of which you have no hope
seek only that

of which you have no clue
love is the sea of not being
and there intellect drowns

this is not the Oxus River
or some little creek
this is the shoreless sea;
here swimming ends
always in drowning

a journey to the sea
is horses and fodder and contrivance

but at land's end
the footsteps vanish

you lift up your robe
so as not to wet the hem;
come! drown in this sea
a thousand times

the moon passes over
the ocean of nonbeing
droplets of spray tear loose
and fall back on the cresting waves

a million galaxies
are a little scum
on that shoreless sea

(translated by Daniel Liebert)

LIKE THIS

If anyone asks you about the houris of paradise,
unveil yourself;
when they speak to you of the moon,
rise over the roof.
If they ask, "What is a peri?",
show them your face;
when they wonder about musk,
scatter your tresses.
"What is it like when the clouds
open up before the moon?"
"Like this," tell them, & button by button
undo your robe.
"How was it that the Messiah
brought life to the dead?" they ask;
Come, kiss me on the lips
& show them.
I told the secret of my union with the friend
to no one but the East Wind
till at last in its mysterious purity
it too whispered, ". . . like this!"
I asked, "How can the fragrance of a Yusuf
be wafted from city to city?"
Then God blew a perfume from the World of Essences
& showed me.
"How can the scent of a Yusuf
open my eyes?"

The breeze touched my face with light
and said, "Like this!"
I am a Court of angels,
my breast an expanse of azure;
come, lift up your eyes & gaze on heaven
& say, "Yes . . . like this!"

(translated by Peter Lamborn Wilson)

Travel

If a tree could get up & walk from place to place it'd never
    suffer saw's pain nor axe's cruel blow—
if Sun & Moon lurked unmoving as solid rock what kind of
    light could they hope to bestow?
How bitter Bactrus River, Tigris, & Euphrates if they stood in
    place sluggish as the Sea;
even Air stagnating in a well becomes a poison murk—can *air*
    suffer loss from delay? Just see:
how when Ocean's moisture travels upon air as cloud it loses
    its load of salt & becomes sweet as cane,
but Fire itself must face ashes, death, & nothingness when
    held back from the motion of blazing flame.
Take Joseph of Canaan: only when he left his father's side &
    traveled to Egypt was he raised above other men—
or Moses: only when he took leave of his mother & set out on
    the road to Midian did he become God's Friend—

or Jesus son of Mary who wandered unceasing as water from
    the Fountain of Youth "which brings life to the dead"*
or Mohammad the messenger who left Mecca behind & only
    returned to rule it at an army's head—
and when he flew upon Boraq in the Night Ascent reached the
    Station of "Nearer Than Two Bows' Length."†
I could make this poem an Encyclopedia of World-Famous
    Travelers—did I not fear to bore you or try your strength!
So take these few for examples & yourself become all the rest,
    my friend.
Journey forth from your own self to God's Self—voyage
    without end.

(translated by Peter Lamborn Wilson)

THE ELEPHANT'S DREAM

There must exist an elephant, so that when
it sleeps by night, it can dream about Hindustan.
After all, the ass can't dream about Hindustan
because the ass has never been there (or never left)—
so there's need of a spirit with the power of an elephant
able to journey in sleep to Hindustan.
Desire makes the elephant remember
Hindustan—
nostalgia by night gives his recollection form;
not just any scoundrel understands *"Remember ye Allah"*;‡

* Qur'an 3:49.
† Qur'an 43:9.
‡ Qur'an 33:41.

"*Return thou*"* is not a chain for just any troublemaker.
But don't give up hope: become an elephant—
or if not quite that, search out a transmutation.
Look: the alchemists of the celestial spheres; listen:
even now sounds come from the laboratory of the Stone
as those architects of the pattern of Heaven
take our affairs in hand.
If you cannot dream of the musk-breasted ones of Hindustan,
if you are night-blind, still you can feel the touch,
their touch, brush your perception; still you can feel
green things springing always fresh from your mortal clay.
Prince Ibrahim ben Adham was one to whom in sleep
the whole of the heart's Hindustan was once unveiled,
causing him to break from the chains of his royalty,
scatter his kingdom to the winds, and vanish.

You will know the man who has dreamed of it
by the way he leaps from sleep like a lunatic,
heaping cinders on all his careful planting,
    springing the trap that has kept him prisoner.

(translated by Peter Lamborn Wilson)

---

* Qur'an 89:28.

· 6 ·

The Gift and the Giver

W HAT DOES NOT COME into man's imagination is called a
"gift" because whatever passes through his imagination is in
proportion to his aspiration and his worth. However, God's gift
is in proportion to God's worth. Therefore, the gift is that which
is suitable to God, not what is suitable to the imagination or
ambition of God's servant. "What no eye has seen nor ear heard
nor has occurred to the mind of man"*—that is, no matter how
much eyes have seen, ears heard, or minds conceived the gift
you expect of Me, My gift is above and beyond all that."

FIHI MA FIHI #31

THIS UNIVERSE IS FOR SATISFYING NEEDS

It was Mary's painful need that made the infant Jesus
begin to speak from the cradle.
Whatever grew has grown for the sake of those in need,
so that a seeker might find the thing she sought.
If God most High has created the heavens,
He has created them for the purpose of satisfying needs.

* The famous divine hadith (a´dadtu li-´ibâdî), "What no eye . . . have I
prepared for my righteous servants."

55

Wherever a pain is, that's where the cure goes;
wherever poverty is, that's where provision goes.
Wherever a difficult question is,
that's where the answer goes;
wherever a ship is, water goes to it.
Don't seek the water; increase your thirst,
so water may gush forth from above and below.
Until the tender-throated babe is born,
how should the milk for it
flow from the mother's breast?

MATHNAWI III, 3204; 3208–3213
(translated by Kabir Helminski and Camille Helminski)

RAMADAN

O moon-faced Beloved,
the month of Ramadan has arrived.
Cover the table
and open the path of praise.

O fickle busybody,
it's time to change your ways.
Can you see the one who's selling the halvah;
how long will it be the halvah you desire?

Just a glimpse of the halvah-maker
has made you so sweet even honey says,
"I'll put myself beneath your feet, like soil;
I'll worship at your shrine."
Your chick frets within the egg

with all your eating and choking.
Break out of your shell that your wings may grow.
Let yourself fly.

The lips of the Master are parched
from calling the Beloved.
The sound of your call resounds
through the horn of your empty belly.

Let nothing be inside of you.
Be empty: give your lips to the lips of the reed.
When like a reed you fill with His breath,
then you'll taste sweetness.

Sweetness is hidden in the Breath
that fills the reed.
Be like Mary—by that sweet breath
a child grew within her.

(translated by Nevit Ergin with Camille Helminski)

Borrowed Clothes

That servant for whom the world lovingly wept
the world now rejects: what did he do wrong?
His crime was that he put on borrowed clothes
and pretended he owned them.
We take them back, in order that he may know for sure
that the stock is Ours and the well-dressed are only
    borrowers;

that he may know that those robes were a loan,
a ray from the Sun of Being.
All that beauty, power, virtue, and excellence
have arrived here from the Sun of Excellence.
They, the light of that Sun, turn back again,
like the stars, from these bodily walls.
When the Sunbeam has returned home,
every wall is left darkened and black.
That which amazed you in the faces of the fair
is the Light of the Sun reflected in the three-colored glass.
The glasses of diverse hue cause the Light to assume color
        for us.
When the many-colored glasses are no longer,
then the colorless Light amazes you.
Make it your habit to behold the Light without the glass,
so that when the glass is shattered you may not be left blind.

MATHNAWI V, 981–991
(translated by Kabir Helminski and Camille Helminski)

THE OWNER OF ALL STATES

"I am only the house of your Beloved,
not the Beloved herself:
true love is for the hidden treasure,
not for the chest that contains it."
The real Beloved is that One who is unique,
who is your beginning and your end.
When you find that One,
you'll no longer want anything else:

that One is both the manifest and the mystery.
That One is the Owner of all states of feeling,
and depends on none:
the months and years are slaves of that moon.
When He bids a "state," it does His bidding;
when that One wills, flesh becomes spirit.

MATHNAWI III, 1417–1421
(translated by Kabir Helminski and Camille Helminski)

THE NET OF GRATITUDE

Giving thanks for abundance
is sweeter than the abundance itself:
Should one who is absorbed with the Generous One
be distracted by the gift?
Thankfulness is the soul of beneficence;
abundance is but the husk,
for thankfulness brings you to the place where the Beloved
    lives.
Abundance yields heedlessness;
thankfulness brings alertness:
hunt for bounty with the net of gratitude.

MATHNAWI III, 2895–2897
(translated by Kabir Helminski and Camille Helminski)

LIVELIHOOD

Trust in God is the best livelihood.
Everyone needs to trust in God
and ask, "O God, bring this work of mine to success."
Prayer involves trust in God, and trust in God
is the only means of livelihood that is independent of all
    others.
In these two worlds I don't know of any means of livelihood
better than trust in our Sustainer.
I know nothing better than gratitude
which brings in its wake the daily bread and its increase.

MATHNAWI V, 2425–2426
(translated by Kabir Helminski and Camille Helminski)

THE DRUNKARDS

The drunkards are rolling in slowly, those who hold to wine
    are approaching.
The lovers come, singing, from the garden, the ones with
    brilliant eyes.

The I-don't-want-to-lives are leaving, and the I-want-to-lives
    are arriving.
They have gold sewn into their clothes, sewn in for those who
    have none.

Those with ribs showing who have been grazing in the old
    pasture of love
are turning up fat and frisky.

The souls of pure teachers are arriving like rays of sunlight
from so far up to the ground-huggers.

How marvelous is that garden, where apples and pears, both
    for the sake of the two Marys,
are arriving even in winter.

Those apples grow from the Gift, and they sink back into the
    Gift.
It must be that they are coming from the garden to the garden.

(translated by Robert Bly)

✦ ✦ ✦

The inner search is from You.
The blind are cured by Your gift.
Without our searching, You gave us this search.

MATHNAWI I, 1337–1338
(translated by Kabir Helminski and Camille Helminski)

✦ ✦ ✦

Know, son, that everything in the universe
is a pitcher brimming with wisdom and beauty.
The universe is a drop of the Tigris of His Beauty,
this Beauty not contained by any skin.
His Beauty was a Hidden Treasure so full
it burst open and made the earth
more radiant than the heavens.

MATHNAWI I, 2860–2862
(translated by Kabir Helminski and Camille Helminski)

· 7 ·

The Passion for God

I KNOW TRULY the rule for God's provision, and it is not in my character to run from pillar to post in vain or to suffer needlessly. Truly whatever my daily portion is—of money, food, clothing, or of the fire of lust—if I sit quietly, it will come to me. If I run around in search of my daily bread, the effort exhausts and demeans me. If I am patient and stay in my place, it will come to me without pain and humiliation. My daily bread is seeking me out and drawing me. When it can't draw me, it comes—just as when I can't draw it, I go to it.

The upshot of these words is that you should be so engaged in the spiritual work that this world will run after you. What is meant by "sitting" here is sitting on the affairs of religion. If a man runs, when he runs for religion he is sitting. If he is sitting, when he is sitting for this world he is running. The Prophet said, "Whoso makes all his cares a single care, God will spare him all his cares."* If a man has ten concerns, let him be concerned with

---

* The full text of the hadith (*man ja´ala 'l-humûm*): "Whoso makes his concerns one concern, God will spare him the concern of this world; but whoso allows his concerns to branch out, God will not care in what valley of this world he perishes."

religion: God will see to the other nine without his having to see to them. The prophets were not concerned with fame or bread. Their only concern was to seek God's satisfaction, and they acquired both fame and bread. Whoever seeks God's satisfaction will be with the prophets in this world and the next; he will be an intimate of *those unto whom God hath been gracious, of the prophets, and the sincere, and the martyrs* [4:69]. What place is this? He will be rather sitting with God, who said, "I sit next to him who remembers Me."* If God were not sitting with him, there would be no desire for God in his heart. Without a rose there is no rose scent; without musk there is no aroma of musk. There is no end to these words, and even if there were it would not be like the end to other words.

FIHI MA FIHI #4

---

* The full text of the hadith qudsi *(ana jalîs)* is given by Munawi, al-Ithafat, p. 110, #254: "Moses said, 'O Lord, are you close enough for me to whisper in your ear or so distant that I should shout?' And God said, 'I am behind you, before you, at your right and your left. O Moses, I am sitting next to my servant whenever he remembers me, and I am with him when he calls me.'"

The Sound of Water in the Ears
of the Thirsty

The real work belongs to someone who desires God
and has severed himself from every other work.

The rest are like children who play together until it gets dark
for these few short days.
Or like someone who awakes and springs up, still drowsy,
and then is lulled back to sleep
by the suggestion of an evil nurse:
"Go to sleep, my darling, I won't let anyone disturb you."

If you are wise, you, yourself,
will tear up your slumber by the roots,
like the thirsty man who heard the noise of the water.

God says to you, "I am the sound of water
in the ears of the thirsty;
I am rain falling from heaven.
Spring up, lover, show some excitement!
How can you hear the sound of water and then fall back
    asleep!"

MATHNAWI VI, 586–592
(translated by Kabir Helminski and Camille Helminski)

* * *

Love of the dead does not last,
because the dead will not return.
But love of the living
is in every moment fresher than a bud,
both to the inward and the outward eye.
Choose the love of that Living One
who is everlasting, who offers you
the wine that increases life.
Do not say, "We have no entrance to that King."
Dealings with the generous are not difficult.

MATHNAWI I, 217–219, 221
(translated by Kabir Helminski and Camille Helminski)

* * *

I am burning.
If anyone lacks tinder,
let him set his rubbish ablaze with my fire.

MATHNAWI I, 1721
(translated by Kabir Helminski and Camille Helminski)

DROWNED IN GOD

Dam the torrent of ecstasy when it runs in flood,
so that it won't bring shame and ruin.
But why should I fear ruin?
Under the ruin waits a royal treasure.
He that is drowned in God wishes to be more drowned.

While his spirit is tossed up and down
by the waves of the sea,
he asks, "Is the bottom of the sea more delightful, or the top?
Is the Beloved's arrow more fascinating, or the shield?"
O heart, if you recognize any difference
between joy and sorrow,
these lies will tear you apart.
Although your desire tastes sweet,
doesn't the Beloved desire you
to be desireless?
The life of lovers is in death:
you will not win the Beloved's heart
unless you lose your own.

MATHNAWI I, 1743–1749, 1751
(*translated by Kabir Helminski and Camille Helminski*)

INTELLIGENCE AND TEARS

Till the cloud weeps, how should the garden smile?
The weeping of the cloud and the burning of the sun
are the pillars of this world: twist these two strands together.
Since the searing heat of the sun and the moisture of the
    clouds
keep the world fresh and sweet,
keep the sun of your intelligence burning bright
and your eye glistening with tears.

MATHNAWI V, 134; 138–139; 141–142
(*translated by Kabir Helminski and Camille Helminski*)

♦ ♦ ♦

In the presence of His Glory,
closely watch your heart
so your thoughts won't shame you.
For He sees guilt, opinion, and desire
as plainly as a hair in pure milk.

MATHNAWI I, 3144–3145
(translated by Kabir Helminski and Camille Helminski)

♦ ♦ ♦

Whatever it is you wish to marry,
go, absorb yourself in that beloved,
assume its shape and qualities.
If you wish for the light, prepare yourself
to receive it; if you wish to be far from God,
nourish your egoism and drive yourself away.
If you wish to find a way out of this ruined prison,
don't turn your head away from the Beloved,
but bow in worship and draw near.

MATHNAWI I, 3605–3607
(translated by Kabir Helminski and Camille Helminski)

Look at yourself, trembling, afraid of nonexistence:
know that nonexistence
is also afraid
that God might bring it into *existence*.
If you grasp at worldly dignities,
it's from fear, too.
Everything, except love of the Most Beautiful,
is really agony. It's agony
to move toward death and not drink the water of life.

MATHNAWI I, 3684–3687
(translated by Kabir Helminski and Camille Helminski)

YOU ARE NOT A SINGLE "YOU"

When you fall asleep,
you go from the presence of yourself
into your own true presence.
You hear something
and surmise that someone else in your dream
has secretly informed you.
You are not a single "you."
No, you are the sky and the deep sea.
Your mighty "Thou," which is nine hundredfold,
is the ocean, the drowning place
of a hundred "thous" within you.

MATHNAWI III, 1300–1303
(translated by Kabir Helminski and Camille Helminski)

The Three States

Human beings have three spiritual states. In the first, a person pays no attention whatsoever to God and worships anything— sex, money, rank—*but* God. When he starts to learn something deeper, then he will serve no one and nothing but God. And when he progresses in this state he grows silent; he doesn't claim: "I don't serve God," nor does he boast: "I do serve God"; he has gone beyond these two positions. From such beings, no sound comes into the world.

(translated by Andrew Harvey)

· 8 ·

Signs That Speak

GOD WORKS IN MYSTERIOUS WAYS. Things may look good outwardly, but there may be evil contained inside. Let no one be deluded by pride that he himself has conceived good ideas or done good deeds. If everything were as it seemed, the Prophet would not have cried out with such illuminated and illuminating perspicacity, "Show me things as they are! You make things appear beautiful when in reality they are ugly; You make things appear ugly when in reality they are beautiful. Show us therefore each thing as it is lest we fall into a snare and be ever errant."

FIHI MA FIHI #1

THE NAME

Do you know a word that doesn't refer to something?
Have you ever picked and held a rose from R,O,S,E?
You say the Name. Now try to find the reality it names.
Look at the moon in the sky, not the one in the lake.
If you want to be free of your obsession with words and
    beautiful lettering, make one stroke down.
There's no self, no characteristics,
but a bright center where you have the knowledge
the Prophets have, without books or interpreter.

(translated by Coleman Barks)

71

With us, the name of everything
is its outward appearance;
with the Creator,
the name of each thing is its inward reality.
In the eye of Moses, the name of his rod was "staff";
in the eye of the Creator, its name was "dragon."
In brief, that which we are in the end
is our real name with God.

MATHNAWI I, 1239–1240, 1244
(translated by Kabir Helminski and Camille Helminski)

You Are an Eye

Since you have perceived the dust of forms,
perceive the wind that moves them;
since you have perceived the foam,
perceive the ocean of Creative Energy.

Come, perceive it, for in you
insight is all that matters;
the rest is just fat and flesh,
a weft and warp of bones and muscle.

Your fat never increased the light in candles;
your flesh never became roast meat
for someone drunk with spiritual wine.
Dissolve this whole body of yours in vision:

pass into sight, pass into sight, pass into sight!
One sight perceives only two yards ahead;
another sight has beheld the two worlds
and the Face of the King.

Between these two
is an incalculable difference:
seek the remedy of vision,
and God best knows that which is hidden.

MATHNAWI VI, 1460–1465
(translated by Kabir Helminski and Camille Helminski)

IN PAIN I BREATHE

In pain, I breathe easier.
The scared child is running from the house, screaming.
I hear the gentleness.

Under nine layers of illusion, whatever the light,
on the face of any object, in the ground itself,
I see your face.

FURUZANFAR #1131
(translated by John Moyne and Coleman Barks)

Everyone Is Dying

Everyone in the world, whether man or woman,
is dying and continually passing through the agony of death.
Regard their words as the final injunctions
which a father gives his son. In this way
consideration and compassion may grow in your heart,
and the root of hatred and jealousy may be cut away.
Look upon your kinsman with that intention,
that your heart may burn with pity for his death agony.
Everything that is coming will come:
consider it to have already arrived;
consider your friend to be already
in the throes of death, losing his life.
If selfish motives prevent you from this insight,
cast them from your heart;
and if you cannot cast them out, don't stand inertly in
    incapacity:
know that with everyone who feels incapable,
there is a goodly Incapacitator.
Incapacity is a chain laid upon you:
you must open your eye to behold the One who lays the chain.

MATHNAWI VI, 761–768
(translated by Kabir Helminski and Camille Helminski)

The Edge of the Roof

I don't like it here, I want to go back.
According to the old Knowers
if you're absent from the one you love
even for one second that ruins the whole thing!

There must be someone . . . just to find
one *sign* of the other world in this town
would be enough.

You know the great Chinese Simurgh bird
got caught in this net . . .
And what can I do? I'm only a wren.
My desire-body, don't come
strolling over this way.
Sit where you are, that's a good place.

When you want dessert, you choose something rich.
In wine, you look for what is clear and firm.
What is the rest? The rest is mirages,
and blurry pictures, and milk mixed with water.
The rest is self-hatred, and mocking other people, and
     bombing.
So just be quiet and sit down.
The reason is—you are drunk,
and this is the edge of the roof.

(translated by Robert Bly)

Water of the Water

Day and night the Sea throws up froth.
You see the foaming surface, but not the Sea. Amazing!
We are dashing against each other like boats:
our eyes are darkened though we're in clear water.
Asleep in the body's skiff, we float,
unaware of the Water of the water.
The water has a Water that is driving it;
the spirit has a Spirit that is calling it.

MATHNAWI III, 1271–1274
(translated by Kabir Helminski and Camille Helminski)

Animal Cookies

God gives the things of this earth
a certain color and variety and value,
causing childish folk to argue over it.

When a piece of dough is baked
in the shape of a camel or lion,
these children bite their fingers excitedly in their greed.

Both lion and camel turn to bread in the mouth,
but it's futile to tell this to children.

MATHNAWI VI, 4717–4719
(translated by Kabir Helminski and Camille Helminski)

Heroes

Does any artist paint for the sake of the picture itself,
without the hope of offering some good?
No, but for the sake of the viewers and the young
who will be drawn by it and freed from cares.
Or does any potter hastily throw a pot or a bowl
without any thought of what it will hold?
Does any calligrapher write for the script alone
without any regard for the reader?
The external form is for the sake of something unseen,
and that took shape for something else unseen.
Just as the moves in a game of chess
reveal the results of each move in what follows.
They make one move to conceal another move,
and that for something else, and so on and on.
So move on, aware of reasons within reasons,
one move after another to checkmate.

One step is for the sake of another,
like the rungs of a ladder, to reach the roof.
The hunger for food produces semen;
semen is for procreation, and the light in the parents' eyes.
Someone with dulled vision sees no further than this:
his intelligence has no movement; it vegetates.
Whether a plant is summoned or not,
it stays planted within the soil.
Don't be deceived if the wind bends it.

Its head says: "We obey the zephyr's request,"
while its feet say, "Leave us alone!"
Since he does not know how to move,
he advances on trust like the blind.
Consider what acting on trust means in a war:
it's like a gambler trusting the throw of the dice.
But if someone's insight is unfrozen, it penetrates the veil.
He sees with his own eye in the present
what will come to pass in ten years' time.
In the same way, everyone sees the unseen and the future,
both good and bad, according to the measure of his insight.
When the barriers in front and behind are removed,
the eye penetrates and reads the Tablet of the Unseen.
When he looks back to the origin of existence,
the beginning and all the past display themselves, including
    the argument between the angels of earth
and the Divine Majesty, their resistance
to recognizing our Father Adam as God's steward.

And when he casts his eye forward,
he sees all that will come to pass until the Gathering.
Therefore he sees back to the root of the root,
and forward to the Day of Decision.
Anyone, to the degree of his enlightenment,
sees as much as he has polished of himself.
The more he polishes, the more he sees,
the more visible do the forms become.
If you say purity is by the grace of God,

this success in polishing is also through that Generosity.
That work and prayer is in proportion to the yearning:
People have nothing but what they have striven for.

God alone is the giver of aspiration:
no rough brute aspires to kingliness,
nor does God's gift of good fortune preclude
one's own consent and will and choice.
But when He brings trouble upon some ill-fated person,
he ungratefully packs off in flight.
Whereas when God brings trouble upon a blessed man,
he just draws nearer to God.
In battle the cowardly, from fear of their lives,
have chosen their means of escape.
But heroes are borne forward by their fear and pain.
From fear, too, the weak soul dies within itself.
Tribulation and fear for one's life are touchstones
to distinguish the cowardly from the brave.

MATHNAWI IV, 2881 AND FOLLOWING
(translated by Kabir Helminski)

· 9 ·

The Pearl of the Heart

"CONSULT YOUR HEART even if the legalist has issued you an opinion."* You have discernment within you. Show the legalist's opinion to that discernment so that it can choose what suits it best. When a physician comes to a sick person he makes inquiries of the "internal physician" you have within you, that is, your temperament, or that which accepts what is good for you and rejects what is bad. Therefore, the external physician inquires of the internal physician as to the quality of what you have eaten, whether it was heavy or light, and how you have been sleeping. The external physician makes his diagnosis based on what the inner physician tells him. The inner physician, the essence, is then the principal one; and when he "falls ill," meaning that the essence becomes corrupt, the result is that he sees things "backward" and describes his symptoms "crooked." He calls sugar sour and vinegar sweet. In this case he is in need of the external physician to help him return to his normal condition, whereupon the external physician can once again take counsel from the internal. Now,

---

* For the prophetic hadith (*istafti qalbaka*) see Furuzanfar's *Ahadith al-Mathnawi* 188 #597.

man also has an inner capacity for discernment; and when it falls ill, whatever his internal senses see or say is contrary to actuality. In this case, the saints are the physicians who help to straighten his essence, and his heart and religion to be strengthened. "Show me things as they are!"*

A human being is a great thing: everything is inscribed within him, but "veils" and "obfuscations" prevent him from reading the knowledge he has within himself. The "veils" and "obfuscations" are various preoccupations, worldly stratagems, and desires. Yet, despite all these things that lie hidden in the "darkness" behind the "veils," a human being does manage to read something and to be aware of what he reads. Consider how "aware" he becomes and what knowledge of himself he discovers when the veils are lifted and the darkness is dissipated. All manner of trades, like tailoring, building, harvesting, goldsmithery, astronomy, medicine—ad infinitum—have been discovered from within man, not from under rocks and mud clumps. It is said that a raven taught man to bury the dead,† but it actually came from a reflection of man cast onto the raven. It was man's own urge that caused him to do it, for, after all, animals are part of man. How can a part teach the whole? Similarly, if man wants to write with his left hand, he may pick

---

* A prophetic hadith (arinâ 'l-ashyâ').

† According to Islamic legend, when Cain killed Abel he did not know what to do with the corpse until two ravens appeared and fought to the death. The victor scratched the earth and dug a hole to bury that dead raven, thereby teaching mankind how to inter the dead. See Qur'an 5:31 and Thackston, *Tales of the Prophets*, p. 78.

up the pen but, no matter how firm his resolve may be, his hand
will still shake as it writes. Nonetheless, the hand does write
something because of the command from the heart.

FIHI MA FIHI #11

ONLY THE HEART

If a wealthy person brings a hundred sacks of gold,
God will only say,
"Bring the Heart, you who are bent double.
If the Heart is pleased with you, I am pleased;
and if the Heart is opposed to you, I am opposed.
I don't pay attention to "you"; I look to the heart:
bring it, poor soul, as a gift to My door!
Its relation to you is also mine:
Paradise is at the feet of mothers."*
The heart is the mother and father and origin of all creatures:
the one who knows the heart from the skin is blessed.
You will say, "Look, I have brought a heart to You."
God will respond, "The world is full of these hearts.
Bring the heart that is the axis of the world
and the soul of the soul of the soul of Adam."
The Ruler of all hearts is waiting
for a heart filled with light and goodness.

MATHNAWI V, 881–888
(translated by Kabir Helminski and Camille Helminski)

---

* *Hadith*, a saying of the Prophet Muhammad.

Why Are You Milking Another?

Strip the raiment of pride from your body:
in learning, put on the garment of humility.
Soul receives from soul the knowledge of humility,
not from books or speech.
Though mysteries of spiritual poverty
are within the seeker's heart,
she doesn't yet possess knowledge of those mysteries.
Let her wait until her heart expands and fills with Light:
God said, "*Did We not expand your breast . . . ?**
For We have put illumination there,
We have put the expansion into your heart."
When you are a source of milk, why are you milking another?
An endless fountain of milk is within you:
why are you seeking milk with a pail?
You are a lake with a channel to the Sea:
be ashamed to seek water from a pool;
for did *We not expand your chest . . . ?*
Again, don't you possess the expansion?
Why are you going about like a beggar?
Contemplate the expansion of the heart within
you, that you may not be reproached with,
Do you not see?†

MATHNAWI V, 1061; 1064–1072
(*translated by Kabir Helminski and Camille Helminski*)

* Qur'an 94:1, Surah Ash-Sharh (Opening of the Heart).
† Qur'an, Surah Adh-Dhariyat (The Dust-Scattering Winds).

The Six-Faced Mirror

The Prophet said, "God doesn't pay attention to your outer
    form:
so in your improvising, seek the owner of the Heart."
God says, "I regard you through the owner of the Heart,
not because of prostrations in prayer
or the giving of wealth in charity."*
The owner of the Heart becomes a six-faced mirror:
through him God looks out upon all the six directions.

MATHNAWI V, 869–870; 874
(translated by Kabir Helminski and Camille Helminski)

＊ ＊ ＊

When your heart becomes the grave of your secret,
that desire of yours will be gained more quickly.
The Prophet said that anyone
who keeps secret his inmost thought
will soon attain the object of his desire.
When seeds are buried in the earth,
their inward secrets become the flourishing garden.

MATHNAWI I, 175–177
(translated by Kabir Helminski and Camille Helminski)

* *Hadith Qudsi,* an extra-Qur'anic revelation.

Someone with a clear and empty heart
mirrors images of the Invisible.
He becomes intuitive and certain
of our innermost thought,
because "the faithful are a mirror for the faithful."

MATHNAWI I, 3146–3147
(translated by Kabir Helminski and Camille Helminski)

+ + +

Know the mirror of the heart is infinite.
Either the understanding falls silent,
or it leads you astray,
because the heart is *with* God,
or indeed the heart *is* He.

MATHNAWI I, 3488–3491
(translated by Kabir Helminski and Camille Helminski)

+ + +

Those with mirrorlike hearts
do not depend on fragrance and color:
they behold Beauty in the moment.
They've cracked open the shell of knowledge
and raised the banner
of the eye of certainty.
Thought is gone in a flash of light.

MATHNAWI I, 3492–3494
(translated by Kabir Helminski and Camille Helminski)

* * *

Just as your two eyes are under the control of the heart
and subject to the spirit's command,
all five senses move as the heart directs.
Hand and foot also move
like the staff in the hand of Moses.
If the heart wills, at once the foot begins to dance,
from neediness toward abundance.

MATHNAWI I, 3562, 3566–3569
(*translated by Kabir Helminski and Camille Helminski*)

* * *

If the heart is restored to health,
and purged of sensuality,
then *The Merciful God is seated on the Throne.*
After this, He guides the heart directly,
since the heart is with Him.

MATHNAWI I, 3665–3666
(*translated by Kabir Helminski and Camille Helminski*)

* * *

Night cancels the business of day;
inertia recharges the mind.
Then the day cancels the night,
and inertia disappears in the light.
Though we sleep and rest in the dark,
doesn't the dark contain the water of life?
Be refreshed in the darkness.

Doesn't a moment of silence
restore beauty to the voice?
Opposites manifest through opposites:
in the black core of the heart
God created the eternal light of love.

MATHNAWI I, 3861–3865
(translated by Kabir Helminski and Camille Helminski)

THE KERNEL AND THE SHELL

When the kernel swells the walnut shell,
or the pistachio, or the almond, the husk diminishes.
As the kernel of knowledge grows,
the husk thins and disappears,
because the lover is consumed by the Beloved.
Since the quality of being sought is the opposite of seeking,
revelation and divine lightning
consume the prophet with fire.
When the attributes of the Eternal shine forth,
the garment of time is burned away.

MATHNAWI III, 1388–1391
(translated by Kabir Helminski and Camille Helminski)

A Word to the Heart

That which God said to the rose,
and caused it to laugh in full-blown beauty,
He said to my heart,
and made it a hundred times more beautiful.

MATHNAWI III, 4129
(translated by Kabir Helminski and Camille Helminski)

The Window within the Soul

During prayer I am accustomed to turn to God like this
and recall the meaning of Muhammad's words,
"the delight felt in the ritual prayer."*
The window of my soul opens,
and from the purity of the unseen world,
the book of God comes to me straight.
The book, the rain of divine grace, and the light
are falling into my house through a window
from my real and original Source.
The house without a window is hell;
to make a window is the essence of true religion.
Don't thrust your ax upon every thicket;
come, use your ax to cut open a window.

MATHNAWI III, 2401–2405
(translated by Kabir Helminski and Camille Helminski)

* The Prophet Muhammad (peace and blessings be upon him) is said to have mentioned this as one of the three things he loved best in the world.

Precious Core

The core of every fruit is better than its rind:
consider the body to be the rind,
and its friend, the spirit, to be the core.
After all, the Human Being has a precious core;
seek it, inspired by the Divine breath.

Mathnawi III, 3417–3418
(translated by Kabir Helminski and Camille Helminski)

Consult Your Own Hearts

The pleasures of this world are delightful
from a distance before the actual test.
Consult your own hearts.*

To follow one's own desires is to flee from God
and to spill the blood of spirituality
in the presence of His justice.

This world is a trap, and desire is its bait:
escape the traps, and quickly
turn your face toward God.

When you have followed this Way,
you have enjoyed a hundred blessings.
When you have gone the opposite way, you have fared ill.

---

* A saying of the Prophet Muhammad.

So the Prophet said, "Consult your own hearts,
even though the religious judge
advises you about worldly affairs."

Abandon desire, and so reveal His Mercy:
you've learned by experience
the sacrifice He requires.

Since you can't escape, be His servant,
and go from His prison into His rose garden.
When you continually keep watch
over your thoughts and actions,

you are always seeing the Justice and the Judge,
though heedlessness may shut your eyes,
still, that doesn't stop the sun from shining.

MATHNAWI VI, 377–384
(translated by Kabir Helminski and Camille Helminski)

· 10 ·

The Yearning

THERE ARE SOME OF GOD'S SERVANTS who approach God via the Qur'an. There are others, the more elite, who come from God only to find the Qur'an here and realize that it is God who has sent it. *We have surely sent it down; and We will certainly preserve the same* [15:9]. The commentators say this is about the Qur'an. This is all well and good, but there is another meaning here, namely: "We have placed in you a substance, a desire to seek, a yearning, of which We are the keeper. We will not suffer it to be wasted and will bring it to fruition. . . ."

Night and day in this world you are searching for rest and peace, but it is not possible to acquire them in this world. Nonetheless, you are not without this quest for even an instant. Any peace you find in this world is as unstable as a passing lightning flash. What kind of lightning? A lightning full of hail, rain, snow, full of tribulation. For example, say someone wants to go to Antalya but takes the road to Caesarea. Although he may never abandon hope of reaching Antalya, it is impossible to get there by the road he has taken. On the other hand, if he does take the Antalya road, though he be lame and weak, eventually he will arrive since that is where the road ends. Since neither the affairs of this world nor the affairs of the next world are accomplished without suffering, then suffer for the next world lest your suffering go for nought.

You say, "O Muhammad, take my religion away, for I find no peace."

"How can our religion turn a person loose before it brings him to the goal?" he will answer.

The story is told of a teacher who was so destitute that during the winter he had nothing but a length of linen. By chance a flood had caught up a bear in the mountains and swept it down with its head under the water. Some children saw the bear's back and cried out: "Teacher, here is a fur coat fallen in the ditch. Since you are cold, take it out." The teacher was in such need and so cold that he jumped into the ditch to get the fur coat. The bear dug its claw into him and held him in the water. The children cried, "Teacher, either bring the fur out or, if you can't, let it go and come out!"

"I've let the fur go," he said, "but it won't let me go! What am I to do?"

How then is yearning for God to let you go? It is a cause for thanks that we are not in our own hands but in God's.

FIHI MA FIHI #26

The Water We Seek

The eye or the spirit that focuses on the transient
falls on its face wherever it goes.
Someone who focuses on the distance,
without knowledge, may see far,
but just as we do in a dream.

Asleep on the bank of a river, lips parched,
you dream you are running toward water.
In the distance you see the water of your desire
and, caught by your seeing, you run toward it.

In the dream you boast,
"I am the one whose heart can see through the veils."
Yet every step carries you further away
toward the perilous mirage.
From the moment you dreamed you set out
you created the distance
from that which had been near to you.
Many set out on a journey
that leads them farther away from their goal.

The intuitive claims of the sleeper are a fantasy.
You, too, are sleepy; but for God's sake,
if you must sleep, sleep on the Way of God,
and maybe some other seeker on the Way
will awaken you from your fantasies and slumber.

No matter how subtle the sleeper's thought becomes,
his dreams will not guide him Home.

Whether the sleeper's thought is twofold or threefold,
it is error multiplying error.

While he dreams of running through the wilderness,
the waves are lapping so near.
While he dreams of the pangs of thirst,
the water is *nearer than his jugular vein.*

MATHNAWI VI, 3226–3241
(translated by Kabir Helminski)

WITH US

Even if you're not a seeker,
still, follow us, keep searching with us.
Even if you don't know how
to play and sing,
you'll become like us;
with us you'll start singing and dancing.

Even if you are Qarun, the richest of kings,
when you fall in love,
you'll become a beggar.
Though you are a sultan, like us you'll become a slave.

One candle of this gathering
is worth a hundred candles; its light is as great.
Either you are alive or dead.
You'll come back to life with us.

Unbind your feet.
Show the rose garden—
start laughing with your whole body,
like a rose, like us.

Put on the mantle for a moment
and see the ones whose hearts are alive.
Then, throw out your satin dresses
and cover yourself with a cloak, like us.

When a seed falls into the ground,
it germinates, grows, and becomes a tree:
if you understand these symbols,
you'll follow us, and fall to the ground, with us.

God's Shams of Tabriz says
to the heart's bud,
"If your eyes are opened,
you'll see the things worth seeing."

(translated by Nevit Ergin with Camille Helminski)

IT WAS ADAM WHO WEPT

Learn from your great-grandfather Adam!
When he lost the union, the tears
that fell from his face made every valley in Ceylon full of
fragrant spices and herbs.
And you still say you cannot choose the road?
The stubborn angel said that.
And he was the one who refused praise to the inner man.
When a human being has experienced the ecstasy, he knows.
He doesn't say, "Please lay out your system of proofs for me."
From the outer layers of the unconscious, logic;
from the inner man, love.

(translated by Robert Bly)

Idle Questions

A person hit a Worker a good strong blow from behind.

The Worker swung around to return it; and the man said:

"Before you hit me, I have a question for you.

Now this is it: that sound: was it made by my hand or your
neck?"

"The pain I am feeling does not give me leave for speculation.

These things are all right to worry about if you're feeling no
pain."

(translated by Robert Bly)

What Is Bounty without a Beggar?

What is bounty without a beggar? Generosity without a
guest?

Be beggar and guest; for beauty is seeking a mirror, water is
crying for a thirsty man.

Hopelessness and need are a tasteful bezel for that ruby. Your
poverty is a Burak;* don't be a coffin riding on other men's
shoulders.

Thank God you hadn't the means or you may have been a
Pharaoh. The prayer of Moses was, *"Lord, I am in need of
Thee!"*

The Way of Moses is all hopelessness and need and it is the
only way to God.

---

* The magical steed that the Prophet Muhammad, peace be upon him,
rode on his Night Journey to the presence of Allah.

From when you were an infant, when has hopelessness ever failed you?

Joseph's path leads into the pit; don't flee across the chessboard of this world, for it is His game and we are checkmate! checkmate!

Hunger makes stale bread more delicious than halvah. Your discomfort is spiritual indigestion; seek hunger and passion and need!

A mouse is a nibbler. God gave him mind in proportion to his needs. Without need God gives nothing.

How will you impress God? You are a hundred thousand dinars in His debt!

A beggar shows his blindness and palsy, he does not say, "*Give me bread, O, people! I am a rich man with granaries and palaces!*"

Bring a hundred sacks of gold and God will say, "*Bring the heart.*"

And if you bring a dead heart carried like a coffin on your shoulders, God will say, "*O, cheat! Is this a graveyard? Bring the live heart! Bring the live heart!*"

If you haven't any knowledge and only opinions, have good opinions about God. This is the way.

If you can only crawl, crawl to Him.

If you cannot pray sincerely, offer your dry, hypocritical, agnostic prayer; for God in His mercy accepts bad coin.

If you have a hundred doubts of God, make them into ninety doubts. This is the way.

O, Seeker! Though you have broken your vows a hundred
 times, come again! Come again! For God has said,
 *"Though you are on high or in the pit consider me, for I am
 the Way."*

(translated by Daniel Liebert)

THE QUEST

Even though you're not equipped,
keep searching:
equipment isn't necessary on the way to the Sustainer.
Whoever you see engaged in search,
become her friend and cast your head in front of her,
for choosing to be a neighbor of seekers,
you become one yourself;
protected by conquerors,
you will, yourself, learn to conquer.
If an ant seeks the rank of Solomon,
don't smile contemptuously upon its quest.
Everything you possess of skill, and wealth, and handicraft,
wasn't it first merely a thought and a quest?

MATHNAWI III, 1445–1449
(translated by Kabir Helminski and Camille Helminski)

By God, Don't Linger

By God, don't linger
in any spiritual benefit you have gained,
but yearn for more—like one suffering from illness
whose thirst for water is never quenched.
This Divine Court is the Plane of the Infinite.
Leave the seat of honor behind;
let the Way be your seat of honor.

MATHNAWI III, 1960–1961
(*translated by Kabir Helminski and Camille Helminski*)

· 11 ·

Praise, Glory

IN THE PRESENCE OF SHAMSI TABRIZI someone said, "I have proven the existence of God, indisputably." The next morning Mevlâna Shamsuddin said, "Last night the angels came down and blessed that man, saying: 'Praise to God, he has proven our God. May God grant him long life. He has done no injury to mortals.'"

O little man, God is a given fact. His existence needs no logical proof. If you must do something, then prove that you yourself have some dignity and rank in His presence. Otherwise He exists without proof. *Nor is there anything which does not celebrate His praise* [17:44]. Of this there is no doubt.

FIHI MA FIHI #21

To praise God is to be purified: when purity arrives, corruption quickly leaves. Opposites flee from each other: night flees when the light dawns. When the pure Name enters the mouth, neither impurity nor sorrow remain. Your awe and love are the rope to catch My gift: beneath every "O Lord" of yours is many a "Here am I" from Me.

MATHNAWI III, 186–188; 197

Banners of Praise

Our fasting is over; it's the feast day of spring!
O dearest guest, welcome; sorrow be gone!
All praise be to God!

O Love once forsaken, abandoned heart be forgotten now;
your Beloved has arrived, and will forever remain.
All praise be to God!

Parting is forever parted; separation is severed at last;
union is united with no more delay:
All praise be to God!

Flight has flown and exile's pain is banished;
distance is now distant; our nest is filled with joy:
All praise be to God!

The moon in the heavens, the rose in the heart, in Love's
    garden,
the King in his palace, proud banners show forth:
All praise be to God!

Life stirs in the root hair; fluid sap spreads in each tiny leaf;
green buds on the branches crown His dominion:
All praise be to God!

Let the despised enemy come, for he'll meet our Defender;
we challenge his approach for now in safety we say:
All praise be to God!

Flood me completely, with the fire of Love's burning,
for now I can bear it and not burn away:
All praise be to God!

For now in certainty, my soul is free,
and all of earth's sadness has dissolved in earth's clay.
All praise be to God!

O chalice overflowing, poured out for these thirsty worlds—
we thank you, we bless you, and drink while we pray:
All praise be to God!

The world lay parched for so long, an open desert,
until the dew glistened, and your breath
came on the wings of morning.
All praise be to God!

As we waited we were longing for Spring's sun
to renew this life of ours.
Today, Jalaluddin's warm breath arrived from the East.
All praise be to God!

(translated by Camille Helminski with William Hastie)

Praising Manners

We should ask God
to help us toward manners. Inner gifts
do not find their way
to creatures without just respect.

If a man or woman flails about, he not only
smashes his house,
he burns the world down.

Your depression is connected to your insolence
and refusal to praise. Whoever feels himself walking
on the path, and refuses to praise—that man or woman
steals from others every day—is a shoplifter!
The sun became full of light when it got hold of itself.
Angels only began shining when they achieved discipline.
The sun goes out whenever the cloud of
not-praising comes.
The moment the foolish angel felt insolent, he heard the door
close.

(translated by Robert Bly)

Love's Apocalypse, Love's Glory

One breath from the breath of the Lover
Would be enough to burn away the world,
To scatter this insignificant universe like grains of sand.
The whole of the cosmos would become a Sea,
And sacred terror rubble this Sea to nothing.
No human being would remain, and no creature;
A smoke would come from heaven; there would be no more
    man or angel.
Out of this smoke, flame would suddenly flash out across
    heaven.
That second, the sky would split apart and neither space nor
    existence remain.
Vast groans would rise up out of the breast of the universe,
    groans mingled with desolate moaning;
And fire eat up water, and water eat up fire.
The waves of the Sea of the Void would drown in their flood
    the horseman of day and night;
The sun itself fades, vanishes, before this flaming out of the
    soul of man.
Do not ask anyone who is not intimate with the secrets
When the Intimate of the Secret Himself cannot answer you.
Mars will lose its swagger, Jupiter burn the book of the world;
The moon will not hold its empire, its joy will be smirched
    with agony.
Mercury will shipwreck in mud, Saturn burn itself to death;
Venus, singer of heaven, play no longer her songs of joy.

The rainbow will flee, and the cup, and the wine;
There will be no more happiness or rapture,
no more wound or cure.
Water will no longer dance with light,
wind no longer sweep the ground;
Gardens no longer abandon themselves to laughter, April's
clouds no longer scatter their dew.
There will be no more grief, no more consolation, no more
"enemy" or "witness."
No more flute or song, or lute or mode, no more high or low
pitch.
Causes will faint away; the cupbearer will serve himself.
The soul will recite: "O my Lord most high!"
The heart will cry out: "My Lord knows best."
Rise up! The Painter of Eternity has set to work one more
time
To trace miraculous figures on the crazy curtain of the world.
God has lit a fire to burn the heart of the universe,
The Sun of God has the East for a heart; the splendor of that
East
Irradiates at all moments the son of Adam: Jesus, son of Mary.

(*translated by Andrew Harvey*)

◆ ◆ ◆

Water and clay, when fed on the breath of Jesus,
spread wings, became a bird and flew.
Your praise of God is a breath
from your body of water and clay.
Make it a bird of paradise
by breathing into it your heart's sincerity.

MATHNAWI I, 866–867
(translated by Kabir Helminski and Camille Helminski)

· 12 ·

The Only One

ALL DESIRES, PREFERENCES, AFFECTIONS, and loves people have for all sorts of things, such as fathers, mothers, friends, the heavens and earth, gardens, pavilions, works, knowledge, food, and drink—one should realize that every desire is a desire for food, and such things are all "veils." When one passes beyond this world and sees that Sovereign without these "veils," then one will realize that all those things were "veils" and "coverings" and that what they were seeking was in reality that One. All problems will then be solved. All the heart's questions and difficulties will be answered, and everything will become clear. God's response is not such that He must answer each and every problem individually. With one answer, all problems are solved. In winter everyone bundles himself up and huddles in a warm place to escape the cold. All plants and trees drop their leaves and fruit because of the biting cold, and they conceal their raiment within themselves lest they suffer from the chill. When spring "answers" them by manifesting itself, all their different "questions" with regard to life, growth, and decay are answered at once: secondary causes disappear. Everything sticks its head out and knows what has caused that wonder.

God has created these "veils" for a good purpose. If He showed His beauty without a veil, we would not be able to bear it or benefit from it, because we are sustained and strengthened indirectly. You see the sun? In its light, we come and go; we see, and we are able to distinguish good from bad. In it, we warm ourselves. Because of it, trees and gardens bear fruit. In its heat, bitter and sour unripe fruits become ripe and sweet. Under its influence, mines of gold, silver, ruby, and sapphire come to be. If this same sun, which is so beneficial indirectly, were to come closer, not only would it give no benefit, but it would cause the whole world and everything in it to burn up and perish. When God manifests Himself through a veil to a mountain, the mountain becomes full of trees and flowers, embellished with greenery. But if He were to manifest Himself without a veil, the mountain would be destroyed and reduced to dust. *But when his Sustainer appeared with glory to the mountain, He reduced it to dust.* [Qur'an 7:143]

FIHI MA FIHI #9

This Bewildering Game

How are you? *How are you?*
Neither "how" nor "what" will understand you.
Except for the Sultan, the one who is beyond "how" and "what,"
no one will be able to understand.

O my Beauty, the universe is illumined by You—
filled with light.
Yet neither the sky nor the earth can see it fully.

A wind moves this blue curtain
but it's not the air blowing through;
it's a wind known only by God.

Do you know who stitches that cloak of joy,
that cloak of grief?
Why does this cloak
think himself different than the one who sews?

Do you know what image shines
in the mirror's heart?
The one who knows
is the one whose heart is pure.

This universe is a banner
that keeps fluttering.
Your heart sees the banner;
your soul thinks it's the air that makes it move.

But the one who knows
how helpless air is

recognizes that everything
is nothing but God.

O God's Shams of Tabriz,
Our Lord has so many tricks up His sleeve;
without your dice, how could the soul
even begin to play this bewildering backgammon game?

translated by Nevit Ergin and Camille Helminski

The Ruby

At breakfast tea a beloved asked her lover,
"Who do you love more, yourself or me?"
"From my head to my foot I have become you.
Nothing remains of me but my name.
You have your wish. Only you exist.
I've disappeared like a drop of vinegar
in an ocean of honey."

A stone which has become a ruby
is filled with the qualities of the sun.
No stoniness remains in it.
If it loves itself, it is loving the sun.
And if it loves the sun, it is loving itself.
There is no difference between these two loves.

Before the stone becomes the ruby, it is its own enemy.
Not one but two exist.
The stone is dark and blind to daylight.
If it loves itself, it is unfaithful: it intensely resists the sun.

If it says "I," it is all darkness.
A pharaoh claims divinity and is brought down.
Hallaj says the same and is saved.
One I is cursed, another I is blessed.
One I is a stone, another a crystal.
One an enemy of the light, the other a reflector of it.
In its inmost consciousness, not through any doctrine,
it is one with the light.
Work on your stony qualities
and become resplendent like the ruby.
Practice self-denial and accept difficulty.
Always see infinite life in letting the self die.
Your stoniness will decrease; your ruby nature will grow.
The signs of self-existence will leave your body,
and ecstasy will take you over.
Become all-hearing like an ear and gain a ruby earring.
Dig a well in the earth of this body,
or even before the well is dug,
let God draw the water up.

Be always at work scraping the dirt from the well.
To everyone who suffers,
perseverance brings good fortune.
The Prophet has said that each prostration of prayer
is a knock on heaven's door.
When anyone continues to knock,
felicity shows its smiling face.

The light which shines in the eye
is really the light of the heart.

The light which fills the heart
is the light of God, which is pure
and separate from the light of intellect and sense.

MATHNAWI I, 1126–1127
(translated by Kabir Helminski)

THE WINDOW BETWEEN HEARTS

Surely there is a window from heart to heart:
they are not separate or far from each other.
Though two earthenware lamps are not joined,
their light mingles.
No lover seeks union without the beloved also seeking;
but the love of lovers makes the body thin as a bowstring,
while the love of loved ones makes them shapely and pleasing.
When the lightning of love for the beloved
has shot into this heart, know that there is love in that heart.
When love for God has been doubled in your heart,
there is no doubt that God has love for you.
No sound of clapping comes forth from only one hand.
The thirsty man is moaning, "O delicious water!"
The water is calling, "Where is the one who will drink me?"
This thirst in our souls is the magnetism of the Water:
We are Its, and It is ours.

MATHNAWI III, 4391–4399
(translated by Kabir Helminski and Camille Helminski)

The Froth and the Sea

The one who regards the foam explains the mystery,
while the one who regards the Sea is bewildered.
The one who regards the foam forms intentions,
while the one who has known the Sea
makes her heart one with the Sea.
The one who regards the froth calculates and reckons,
while the one who regards the Sea is without conscious
    volition.
The one who regards the froth is continually in motion,
while the one who regards the Sea is free of hypocrisy.

MATHNAWI V, 2908–2911
(translated by Kabir Helminski and Camille Helminski)

The Sea within the Fish

A human being is essentially an eye;
the rest is merely flesh and skin:
whatever the eye has beheld, he is that.
A jar will submerge a mountain with its water
when the eye of the jar is open to the Sea.
When the interior of the jar has a channel to the Sea,
that jar will overwhelm a river as great as the Oxus.
In the same way whatever speech Muhammad uttered,
those words were really uttered by the Sea.
All his words were pearls of the Sea,
for his heart had a passage into that Sea.

Since the bounty of the Sea is poured through our jar,
why should anyone be amazed that the Sea itself
should be contained in a Fish?*

MATHNAWI VI, 812–817
(translated by Kabir Helminski and Camille Helminski)

WATER AND WINE

With Your sweet Soul, this soul of mine
has merged as water does with wine.
Who can part the water from the wine,
or me from You when we combine?

You have become my greater self;
how can smallness limit me?
You've taken on my being,
how shall I not take on Yours?

Forever, You have claimed me
that forever I may know You're mine.
Your love has pierced me to the depths,
its ecstasy entwines both bone and nerve.

I rest as a *ney* laid upon Your lips;
as an *oud* I lie against Your breast.
Breathe deeply in me that I may sigh;
Strike upon my strings and tears glisten.
Sweet are my tears and sweet my sighs;

* The Perfect Human Being

worldly joys I return to the world.
You remain in my inmost Soul
whose depths the mirrored heavens reflect.

O pearl in this mussel shell:
O diamond in my darkest mine!
In You, this honey is dissolved,
O milk of life, so mild, so fine!

Our sweetnesses, all merged in You,
sweeten infant smiles.
You crush me into rose oil, drop by drop;
nor do I complain beneath the press.

In Your sweet pain, pain dissolves;
for I, Your rose, had this intent.
You bade me blossom on Your robe,
and made me for all eyes Your sign.
And when You pour me upon this world,
it blooms in Beauty, fully Divine.

(translated by Camille Helminski with William Hastie)

The Elusive Ones

They're lovers again: sugar dissolving in milk.
Day and night, no difference. The sun is the moon:
An amalgam. Their gold and silver melt together.
This is the season when the dead branch and the green
branch are the same branch.

The cynic bites his finger because he can't understand.
Omar and Ali on the same throne, two kings in one belt.
Nightmares fill with light like a holiday.
Men and angels speak one language.
The elusive ones finally meet.

The essence and the evolving forms
run to meet each other like children
to their father and mother.
Good and evil, dead and alive, everything blooms
from one natural stem.
You know this already, I'll stop.
Any direction you turn it's one vision.
Shams, my body is a candle touched with fire.

Furuzanfar #810
(translated by John Moyne and Coleman Barks)

ONE, ONE, ONE

The lamps are different,
But the Light is the same.
So many garish lamps in the dying brain's lamp shop,
Forget about them.
Concentrate on essence, concentrate on Light.
In lucid bliss, calmly smoking off its own holy fire,
The Light streams toward you from all things,
All people, all possible permutations of good, evil, thought,
    passion.
The lamps are different,
But the Light is the same.
One matter, one energy, one Light, one Light-mind,
Endlessly emanating all things.
One turning and burning diamond,
One, one, one.
Ground yourself, strip yourself down,
To blind loving silence.
Stay there, until you see
You are gazing at the Light
With its own ageless eyes.

(translated by Andrew Harvey)

The clear bead at the center changes everything.
There are no edges to my loving now.
I've heard it said there's a window that opens
from one mind to another,
but if there's no wall, there's no need
for fitting the window, or the latch.

FURUZANFAR #511
(translated by John Moyne and Coleman Barks)

· 13 ·

Boiling the Chickpeas

Say "God" once and stand firm, for all calamities will rain down upon you. Someone once came to the Prophet and said, "I love you."

"Be careful of what you are saying," said the Prophet.

Again the man repeated, "I love you."

"Be careful of what you are saying," the Prophet warned again.

But a third time he said, "I love you."

"Now stand firm," said the Prophet, "for I shall kill you by your own hand. Woe unto you!"

In the time of the Prophet someone said, "I don't want this religion. By God, I don't want it! Take this religion back. Ever since I entered into this religion of yours I have not had one day of peace. I have lost my wealth; I have lost my wife; I have no children left; I have no honor, strength, or passion left."

The reply was, "Wherever our religion goes, it does not come back until it has plucked one out by the roots and swept his house clean." *None shall touch the same, except those who are clean* [56:79].

So long as you have an iota of self-love left within you, no beloved would pay any attention to you. Neither would you be worthy of union nor would any beloved grant you admittance. One must become totally indifferent to the self and inimical to the world in order for the Beloved's Face to be seen. Now, our religion will not let go of a heart that has found stability until it brings it to God and divorces it from everything that is unsuitable. The Prophet said the reason you find no peace and constantly grieve is because grieving is like vomiting. So long as any of those original joys remain in your stomach, you will not be given anything to eat. While a person is vomiting, he cannot eat anything. When he has finished vomiting, then he can eat. You too must wait and suffer grief, for grieving is vomiting. After the vomiting is over, a joy will come that has no grief, a rose that has no thorns, a wine that causes no hangover. Night and day in this world you are searching for rest and peace, but it is not possible to acquire them in this world. Nonetheless, you are not without this quest for even an instant. Any peace you find in this world is as unstable as a passing lightning flash. What kind of lightning? A lightning full of hail, rain, snow, full of tribulation.

FIHI MA FIHI #17

BOIL NICELY NOW

Look at the chickpea in the pot,
how it leaps up when it feels the fire.
While boiling, it continually rises to the top
and cries, "Why are you setting the fire under me?
Since you bought me, why are you turning me upside down?"
The housewife keeps hitting it with the ladle.

"No!" she says, "boil nicely now,
and don't leap away from the one who makes the fire.
It's not because you are hateful to me that I boil you,
but so that you might gain flavor,
and become nutritious and mingle with essential spirit.
This affliction is not because you are despised.
When you were green and fresh,
you were drinking water in the garden;
that water-drinking was for the sake of this fire."

MATHNAWI III, 4159–4165
(*translated by Kabir Helminski and Camille Helminski*)

BUTTERMILK

These creatures of the world exist
to manifest the divine treasure.
God said, "I was a hidden treasure."
Listen, don't let your substance be wasted.
Become manifest!
Your true sincerity is hidden in falsehood,
like the taste of butter in buttermilk.
For years this buttermilk, which is the body,
is obvious and manifest, while the butter,
which is spirit, has disappeared within it.
Until Truth sends a messenger, a servant,
a shaker of the buttermilk in the churn,
who has the skill and the method for churning,
so that I may discover that my true self was hidden.
Or until the words of a servant of that messenger

enter the ear of one who is seeking inspiration.
The ear of the faithful retains the inspiration,
because such an ear is close to the caller,
just as an infant's ear is filled with its mother's words
until it learns to speak.
And if the infant's ear is not right,
it fails to hear its mother's words and is mute.
Anyone born deaf remains mute.
Only one who hears the mother's words learns to speak.
Know that this deafness is a defect,
for the deaf ear does not hear the words and so cannot learn.
Only God, whose attributes are perfect,
possessed speech without being taught.
And Adam whom God taught without
a mother or nurse between,
or the Messiah who was taught by Love
and came into the world with the Word,
so that he could defend himself
from accusations of an illegitimate birth.
A lot of shaking is needed
for the buttermilk to offer up the butter from its heart.
The butter is as invisible as nonexistence itself,
while the buttermilk has raised its own banner in the world.
What seems most to exist is just the skin
of something which seems not to exist but is the source.
If the buttermilk has not yet offered its butter,
store it away until you can extract the butter.
Churn it from side to side, hand to hand,

until it reveals what is hidden within it.
For this perishable body is the evidence of the eternal,
and the babbling of the drunkard
is proof that someone poured the wine.

MATHNAWI IV, 3030 . . .
(*translated by Kabir Helminski*)

+ + +

The spiritual path wrecks the body
and afterward restores it to health.
It destroys the house to unearth the treasure,
and with that treasure builds it better than before.

MATHNAWI I, 306–307
(*translated by Kabir Helminski and Camille Helminski*)

Love Is Like a Lawsuit

I am amazed at the seeker of purity
who when it's time to be polished
complains of rough handling.
Love is like a lawsuit:
to suffer harsh treatment is the evidence;
when you have no evidence, the lawsuit is lost.
Don't grieve when the Judge demands your evidence;
kiss the snake so that you may gain the treasure.
That harshness isn't toward you,
but toward the harmful qualities within you.
When someone beats a rug,
the blows are not against the rug,
but against the dust in it.

MATHNAWI III, 4008–4012
(*translated by Kabir Helminski and Camille Helminski*)

Treasure in the Ruins

Demolish this house, for a thousand houses
may be made from this carnelian.
A treasure lies beneath the house,
So don't stand still, for there is no other way.
Don't be afraid of destroying the house,
because with its treasure in hand you can build
a thousand houses without toil and pain.
In the end this house will fall into ruin,
and the treasure beneath it will be revealed;
But it won't be yours,
since your soul receives that divine gift
as wages for destroying the house.
If it hasn't done the hard work, it earns nothing:
There is nothing for the human being hereafter
but recompense for that which she has wrought here. *

MATHNAWI IV, 2540–2545
(*translated by Kabir Helminski and Camille Helminski*)

---

* Qur'an 3:25, Surah Al-Imran (The House of Imran).

Like Sunlight upon the Earth

I am from you, and at the same time,
you have devoured me.
I melt in you since through you I froze.
You squeeze me with your hand,
and then you step on me with your foot.
This is how the grape becomes wine.

We are cast like sunlight upon the earth.
And our light, passing through the body
as if it were an open window to our Source,
returns, purified, to you.
Whoever sees that sun says,
"He is alive,"
and whoever sees only the window says,
"He is dying."

Our Creator has veiled our origin in that cup of pain and joy.
Within our core we are pure;
all the rest is dregs.
Source of the soul of souls, Shams, the Truth of Tabriz,
a hundred hearts are afire for you.

Furuzanfar #2399
(translated by Kabir Helminski)

The Shop

Lightning falling on the helpless, a surge of pearl out of the
    rock
covering the rock, this life torn into a hundred pieces,
and one of those pieces a ticket
to let me back into my life.

A spirit world divided into eight sections, one a scroll.
Eight scrolls in the parchment of your face.
What kind of bird am I becoming, kneeling like a camel,
pecking at the fire like an ostrich?

You and I have worked in the same shop for years.
Our loves are great fellow workers.
Friends cluster there and every moment we notice
a new light coming out in the sky.
Invisible, yet taking form, like Christ coming through
Mary. In the cradle, God.

Shams, why this inconsistency?
That we live within love
and yet we run away?

FURUZANFAR #2788
(*translated by Coleman Barks*)

· 14 ·

The Complete Human

CONSIDER HOW WOOL IS TURNED into an elegantly designed carpet by coming into contact with an intelligent person. See how dirt can be turned into a fine palace by coming into contact with an intelligent person. If association with the intelligent has such an effect on inanimate objects, think what effect there will be when one seeker of God associates with another. . . . God's saints have witnessed heavens beyond the heavens we know. These heavens are too insignificant to enter their gaze. They have put these heavens beneath their feet and passed them by.

Why should it be strange for an exceptional person among humanity to have developed the ability to place his foot on the seventh heaven? Were we not all of the same nature as the earth? Nonetheless, God placed within us a power by means of which we were elevated above and given control of our nature to do with as we intend.

Sometimes we raise it up, and sometimes we put it down. Sometimes we turn it into buildings, and sometimes we turn it into pots and jugs. Sometimes we lengthen it, and sometimes we shorten it. Although we were at first of the very earth and the same nature as it, God elevated us through that power. Now, why should it be strange if God elevates one of our species, in relation to whom we are like inanimate objects? He has control and is aware of us, while we are unaware of him.

The sheikh is the root of spiritual joy. The oceans of joy are with him. How could he harbor hatred or selfish interests with regard to anyone? God forbid! He speaks out of compassion and empathy about all God's servants. What other interest could he possibly have in these "locusts" and "frogs"? What are these beggars in relation to one who possesses such magnanimity?

Is it not said that the Water of Life is in dark earth? The darkness is the body of the saints, where the Water of Life is. The Water of Life can be found only in the darkness. If you hate the darkness and find it distasteful, how will you find the Water of Life? . . . In order to succeed in learning anything worthwhile, wouldn't you have to endure sufferings and acts contrary to your will? How then would it be if you were to want to acquire eternal, everlasting life, which is the station of the saints? Do you think that in that case you would not suffer anything you dislike, or have to abandon anything you possess? . . . But you won't tolerate the simplest thing you are advised to do. You may hate something even if it is good for you.

What do these people think? They have been stricken by blindness and ignorance. They do not consider how a person in love with a man or a woman may grovel and fawn and sacrifice all his wealth, or how he may beguile his beloved by spending his all in order to placate him or her. He may weary of other things, but of this pursuit he never wearies. Is the sheikh's love—or God's love—less than this? Yet at the least command or advice he turns away and abandons the sheikh. By such action it is understood that he was no lover or aspirant, for, had he been either, he would have endured what we have said many times over, for his heart's dung would have become honey and sugar.

FIHI MA FIHI #63

THE SPIRITUAL SURGEON

Can the water of a polluted stream
Wash away the dirt?
Can human knowledge sweep away
the ignorance of the sensual self?
How does a sword fashion its own hilt?
Go, entrust your wound to a surgeon,
for flies will gather around the wound
until it can't be seen.
These are your selfish thoughts
and all you dream of owning.
The wound is your own dark hole.

MATHNAWI I, 3221–3224
(translated by Kabir Helminski and Camille Helminski)

Feed your heart in conversation
with someone harmonious with it;
seek spiritual advancement from one who is advanced.

MATHNAWI I, 726
(translated by Kabir Helminski and Camille Helminski)

COMPANIONSHIP WITH THE HOLY

Don't take a wooden sword into battle.
Go, find one of steel;
then march forward with joy.

The saint's protection is Truth's sword:
your time with him
is worth as much as the cup of life itself.

All the wise have said the same:
the one who knows God
is God's mercy to His creatures . . .

Companionship with the holy makes you one of them.
Though you're rock or marble, you'll become a jewel
when you reach the man of heart.

Plant the love of the holy ones within your spirit;
don't give your heart to anything,
but the love of those whose hearts are glad.

Don't go to the neighborhood of despair:
there is hope.
Don't go in the direction of darkness:
suns exist.

MATHNAWI I, 714–717, 721–724
(translated by Kabir Helminski and Camille Helminski)

+ + +

Whatever knowledge the master is known to have,
with it the souls of his pupils are imbued.

MATHNAWI I, 2829
(translated by Kabir Helminski and Camille Helminski)

+ + +

O brother, Wisdom is pouring into you
from the beloved saint of God.
You've only borrowed it.
Although the house of your heart
is lit from inside,
that light is lent by a luminous neighbor.
Give thanks; don't be arrogant or vain;
pay attention without self-importance.
It's sad that this borrowed state
has put religious communities
far from religious communion.

MATHNAWI I, 3255–3258
(translated by Kabir Helminski and Camille Helminski)

That Journeys Are Good

If a fir tree had a foot or two like a turtle, or a wing,
do you think it would just wait for the saw to enter?

You know the sun journeys all night under the earth;
if it didn't, how would the cabbages be fed with the rain?

Have you thought of Joseph lately? Didn't he leave his father
    in tears, going?
Didn't he then learn how to understand dreams, and give away
    grain?

And that man with the long nose, didn't he leave his country,
    forced to,
and only then learned how to travel through the three worlds?

And you, if you can't leave your country, you could go into
    yourself.
And become a ruby mine, open to the gifts of the sun.

You could travel from your manhood into the inner man, or
    from your womanhood into the inner woman—
by a journey of that sort earth became a place where you find
    gold.

So leave your complaints and self-pity and internalized death-
    energy.
Don't you realize how many fruits have already escaped out of
    sourness into sweetness?

A good source of sweetness is a teacher, mine is named Shams.
You know every fruit grows more handsome in the light
    of the sun.

(translated by Robert Bly)

LONGING FOR THE BIRDS OF SOLOMON

Is this Stuff poetry? It's what birds sing in cages.
Where are the words spoken by the birds of Solomon?

How would you know their cries, if you heard them,
when you haven't seen Solomon even for two seconds?

That bird lifts his wings, one tip touches East, one West.
Those who hear the note feel an intensity in their whole body.

The bird descends from the Holy One's bedroom door to
    earth,
and from earth it flies among light back to the Great Seat.

Without Solomon every bird is a bat in love with darkness.
Listen, oh mischievous bat, try to become his friend—do you
    want to stay in your cave forever?

If you go even three feet toward Solomon's mountain,
others will use that as a yardstick to measure their lives.

If your leg is gimpy, and you have to hop, what's the difference?
Going there, even by limping, the leg grows whole.

(translated by Robert Bly)

Two Kinds of Miracles

Miracles secret and open
   flow from the teacher.
With reason—that's not unusual at all.
And the tiniest of these miracles
is this: everyone near a saint gets drunk with God.

When a spiritual man lets the water hold up his feet
we are moved, because by ways we cannot see
the sight of that links
the soul back to the source of all lightness.

Of course a saint can move a mountain!
But who cares about that? How marvelous is the bread
made without dough, the dishes of food
that are invisible. Mary's grapes that never saw the vine!

(translated by Robert Bly)

You Embrace Some Form

you embrace some form
saying, *"I am this."*

By God, you are not this
or that or the other

you are *"Unique One"*
"Heart-ravishing"

you are throne and palace and king
you are bird and snare and fowler

like water in jar and river
are in essence the same

you and spirit are the same

your every idol
prostrates
before you

your every thought-form
perishes
in your formlessness

(translated by Daniel Liebert)

· 15 ·

Surrender

W<small>HEN A MAN ACKNOWLEDGES</small> his servanthood in relation to God, he is aware of his act of being a servant. It may be for God, but he still sees himself and his own act along with seeing God. He is not "drowned"; someone is drowned when there is no motion or action, in whom there is no movement but the movement of the water.

A lion chases a gazelle. The gazelle flees from the lion. There are two existences, the lion's and the gazelle's. When the lion catches the gazelle and the gazelle faints in fear under the lion's wrathful paw, then there remains only the lion's existence: the gazelle's being is obliterated.

The saints' "absorption" is such that God causes them to fear Him with a fear different from the fear humans have of lions, tigers, and tyrants. He reveals to them that fear is from God, security is from God, pleasure and ease are from God, and the necessities of day-to-day life are from God. To the saints God appears in a particular, sensible form that can be seen with the eye, like that of a lion, a tiger, or fire. It is apparent to the saint that the lion or tiger's form he is seeing is not of this world but rather an "imaginal" form, one that has been given shape: it is God revealing himself in a form of exquisite beauty. Gardens, camels, houris, mansions, food and drink, robes of honor, cities, houses, and various wonders are the same: the saint knows that none of these is of this world, but God has made them visible by dressing them in form. He knows for certain that fear is from God, security is from God, and all serenity and beautiful things are from God. Now, although the saint's "fear" does not resemble ordinary fear, it can be glimpsed through ordinary fear. It cannot be proven logically. The concept of everything's being from God is bestowed by God.

FIHI MA FIHI #11

SAY YES QUICKLY

Forget your life. Say *God is Great*. Get up.
You think you know what time it is. It's time to pray.
You've carved so many little figurines, too many.
Don't knock on any random door like a beggar.
Reach your long hands out to another door, beyond where
you go on the street, the street
where everyone says, "How are you?"
and no one says *How aren't you?*

Tomorrow you'll see what you've broken and torn tonight,
thrashing in the dark. Inside you
there's an artist you don't know about.
He's not interested in how things look different in moonlight.

If you are here unfaithfully with us,
you're causing terrible damage.
If you've opened your loving to God's love,

you're helping people you don't know
and have never seen.

Is what I say true? Say *yes* quickly,
if you know, if you've known it
from before the beginning of the universe.

FURUZANFAR #2933
(*translated by Coleman Barks*)

GROWING A COAT OF MAIL

Light going dim. Is it my eyes, or a cloud, or the sun
itself, or the window? I can't see the point
of the needle, or the other end of the thread.

I want that moment again when I spread out
like olive oil in the skillet.
The same heat makes iron steel. Abraham,
a bed of jasmine sitting quietly, or talking.

Unmanned, I'm a true person,
or at least the ring knocker on the door where they live.
The Prophet says, *Fasting protects*. Do that.
On dry land a fish needs to be wrapped in something.
In the ocean, as you see, it grows a coat of mail.

FURUZANFAR #1850
(*translated by Coleman Barks*)

Keeper of Secrets

You came here to tell my secret to everyone, what I give
no sign of. Last night in a dream you offered
a cup. I said, I will not drink wine.
Do not, the loss is yours.
I'm afraid of being shamed. I'll reach for you
and you won't be there. *It's astonishing to me
that someone offers you his innermost life, and you frown.
Would you be deceptive with me as you are with others?
I am the Keeper of Secrets. You can't hide from me.
I am the beauty of the perceived world, but you lay back
on the ground. I am the true direction of the spirit,
but you glance around at clouds.*

Look here. If you angrily turn away now,
you will do the same on the day you die. Be pale
for the One who created color. Don't put saffron
on your face for the sake of shadows.
Be a rooster, conscious of time and the leader.
Don't change your rooster to a hen.
Bend and sit crookedly, but tell the straight truth.
Truth is enough. I am the Friend, your spirit.
Why look for someone else?
*If you like the verse about lending to God, lend a clipping
from a counterfeit coin and get back the deed to a diamond mine.
If for two or three days you bandage your eyes with awe,
you make your sensible eyes a fountain for the other ocean.
If for only a second you go straight for this target,*

that arrowy intention becomes your bow and bowstring.
There's no generosity better than this: that with your sins
and forgetfulness I'm telling you how to pray.

So much for words which have to be written down,
or not contained in the mouth. If you were to open
every living particle, you could make a mouth of each.

Furuzanfar #2465
(translated by Coleman Barks)

Whispers of Love

Love whispers in my ear,
"Better to be a prey than a hunter.
Make yourself My fool.
Stop trying to be the sun and become a speck!
Dwell at My door and be homeless.
Don't pretend to be a candle, be a moth,
so you may taste the savor of Life
and know the power hidden in serving."

Mathnawi V, 411–414
(translated by Kabir Helminski)

RIPENED FRUIT

This world is a tree to which we cling—
we, the half-ripe fruit upon it.
The immature fruit clings tight to the branch
because, not yet ripe, it's unfit for the palace.
When fruits become ripe, sweet, and juicy,
then, biting their lips, they loosen their hold.
When the mouth has been sweetened by felicity,
the kingdom of the world loses its appeal.
To be tightly attached to the world is immaturity;
as long as you're an embryo,
blood-sipping is your interest.

MATHNAWI III, 1293–1297
(translated by Kabir Helminski and Camille Helminski)

STAY CLOSE, MY HEART

Stay close, my heart, to the one who knows your ways;
Come into the shade of the tree that always has fresh flowers.
Don't stroll idly through the bazaar of the perfume-makers;
Stay in the shop of the sugar-seller.
If you don't find true balance, anyone can deceive you;
Anyone can trick out of a thing of straw, and make you take it
    for gold.
Don't squat with a bowl before every boiling pot;
In each pot on the fire you find very different things.
Not all sugarcanes have sugar, not all abysses a peak;
Not all eyes possess vision, not every sea is full of pearls.
O nightingale, with your voice of dark honey! Go on
    lamenting!
Only your drunken ecstasy can pierce the rock's hard heart!
Surrender yourself, and if you cannot be welcomed by the
    Friend,
Know that you are rebelling inwardly like a thread
That doesn't want to go through the needle's eye!
The awakened heart is a lamp; protect it by the hem of your
    robe!
Hurry and get out of this wind, for the weather is bad.
And when you've left this storm, you will come to a fountain;
You'll find a Friend there who will always nourish your soul.
And with your soul always green, you'll grow into a tall tree
Flowering always with sweet light-fruit, whose growth is
    interior.

(translated by Andrew Harvey)

The Only Certain Refuge

Really to experience the Day of Resurrection
You have to die first, for "resurrection" means
"Making the dead come back to life."
The whole world is racing in the wrong direction
For everyone is terrified of nonexistence.
That is, in reality, the only certain refuge.
How should we try to win real awareness?
By renouncing all-knowing.
How should we look for salvation?
By giving up our personal salvation.
How should we search for real existence?
By giving up our existence.
How should we search for the fruit of the spirit?
By not always greedily stretching out our hands.

(translated by Andrew Harvey)

Why Cling

Why cling to one life
till it is soiled and ragged?

The sun dies and dies
squandering a hundred lives
every instant

God has decreed life for you
and He will give
another and another and another.

(translated by Daniel Liebert)

Love Is the Master

Love is the One who masters all things;
I am mastered totally by Love.
By my passion of love for Love
I have ground sweet as sugar.
O furious Wind, I am only a straw before you;
How could I know where I will be blown next?
Whoever claims to have made a pact with Destiny
Reveals himself a liar and a fool;
What is any of us but a straw in a storm?
How could anyone make a pact with a hurricane?
God is working everywhere his massive Resurrection;
How can we pretend to act on our own?
In the hand of Love I am like a cat in a sack;
Sometimes Love hoists me into the air,
Sometimes Love flings me to the ground.
Love swings me round and round His head;
I have no peace, in this world or any other.
The Lovers of God have fallen in a furious river;
They have surrendered themselves to Love's commands.
Like mill wheels they turn, day and night, day and night,
Constantly turning and turning, and crying out.

(translated by Andrew Harvey)

You Suspect This Could Be Yours

you suspect this could be yours
with a little contrivance

only death to contrivance
will avail you

something good or bad
always comes out of you
it is agony to be still;
the spool turns
when mind pulls the thread

let the water settle;
you will see moon and stars
mirrored in your being

when the kettle boils
fire is revealed
when the millstone turns
the river shows its power

put the lid on the kettle
and be filled
with the boiling of love.

(translated by Daniel Liebert)

Out of Control

If I had any judgment and skill of my own,
my consideration and plans would all be under my control.

At night my consciousness would not leave against my will,
and the birds of my senses
would be secured within my own cage.

I would be aware of the stages journeyed by the soul
in unconsciousness, in sleep, and in times of trouble.

But since my hand is made empty
by His sovereign power to loosen and to bind,

O, I wonder,
from whom comes this self-conceit of mine?

MATHNAWI VI, 2324–2327
(*translated by Kabir Helminski*)

✦ ✦ ✦

It suits the generous man to give money,
but truly the generosity of the lover
is to surrender his soul.
If you give bread for God's sake,
you will be given bread in return;
if you give your life for God's sake,
you will be given Life in return.

MATHNAWI I, 2235–2236
(*translated by Kabir Helminski and Camille Helminski*)

God's Slave Is Free

The sea doesn't let the fish escape,
nor does it let in the creatures of the land.
The fish swims in its watery home;
the weighty animal plods upon the earth.
Nothing we do can change this.
The lock of Divine destiny is strong,
and the only opener is God.

Cling to surrender and contentment with God's will.
Though the atoms, one by one, should become keys,
nothing is opened except by divine Majesty.
When you forget your own scheming,
happiness will come to you from your spiritual guide.
When you forget your self,
you are remembered by God.

When you have become His slave,
only then are you set free.

MATHNAWI III, 3071–3076
(*translated by Kabir Helminski*)

THE ONE-WAY PULL

O my Sustainer.
deliver me from this imprisonment of free will.
The one-way pull on *the straight Path**
is better than the two-way pull of perplexity.
Though You are the only goal of these two ways,
still this duality is agonizing to the spirit.

Though the destination of these two ways is You alone,
still the battle is never like the banquet.
Listen to the explanation God gave in the Qur'an:
they shrank from bearing it.†
This perplexity in the heart is like war:
when a man is perplexed he says,
"I wonder whether this is better for my situation or that."

In perplexity the fear of failure and the hope of success
always are in conflict with each other, advancing, retreating.
From You came this ebb and flow within me;
otherwise this sea of mine would be still.
From that source from which You gave me this perplexity,
likewise now, graciously give me clarity.

MATHNAWI VI, 203–211
(translated by Kabir Helminski and Camille Helminski)

* Qur'an 1:6, Surah Al-Fatihah (The Opening).
† Qur'an 33:72, Surah Al-Azhab (The Confederates).

· 16 ·

Love Is the Cause

In this world everyone is preoccupied with something. Some are preoccupied with love for women, some with possessions, some with making money, some with learning—and each one believes that his well-being and happiness depend on that. And that also is God's mercy. When a man goes after it in search and does not find it, he turns his back on it. After pausing a while he says: "That joy and mercy must be sought. Maybe I did not look enough. Let me search again." When he seeks again he still does not find it, but he continues until the mercy manifests itself unveiled. Only then does he realize that he was on the wrong track before. God, however, has some servants who see clearly even before the Resurrection. Ali said, "If the veil were lifted I would not be more certain." By this he meant that if the shell were taken away and the Apocalypse were to appear, his certitude would not increase. His perception was like a group of people who go into a dark room at night and pray, each facing a different direction. When day breaks they all turn themselves around, all except the one man who had been facing Mecca all night long. Since the others now turn to face his direction, why should he turn around? Those servants of God face Him even during the night: they have turned away from all that is other than Him. For them the Resurrection is immediate and present.

In a human being is such a love, a pain, an itch, a desire that, even if he were to possess a hundred thousand worlds, he would not rest or find peace. People work variously at all sorts of callings, crafts, and professions, and they learn astrology and medicine, and so forth, but they are not at peace because what they are seeking cannot be found. The beloved is called *dil-ârâm** because the heart finds peace through the beloved. How then can it find peace through anything else? All these other joys and objects of search are like a ladder. The rungs on the ladder are not places to stay but to pass through. The sooner one wakes up and becomes aware, the shorter the long road becomes and the less one's life is wasted on these "ladder rungs."

FIHI MA FIHI #15

---

* *Dil-ârâm*, literally, "that which gives the heart repose," a common term for the beloved.

Song of the Reed

Listen to the reed and the tale it tells,
how it sings of separation:
Ever since they cut me from the reed bed,
my wail has caused men and women to weep.

I want a heart that is torn open with longing
so that I might share the pain of this love.
Whoever has been parted from his source
longs to return to that state of union.

At every gathering I play my lament.
I'm a friend to both happy and sad.
Each befriended me for his own reasons,
yet none searched out the secrets I contain.

My secret is not different than my lament,
yet this is not for the senses to perceive.
The body is not hidden from the soul,
nor is the soul hidden from the body,
and yet the soul is not for everyone to see.

This flute is played with fire, not with wind,
and without this fire you would not exist.
It is the fire of love that inspires the flute.
It is the ferment of love that completes the wine.

The reed is a comfort to all estranged lovers.
Its music tears our veils away. Have you
ever seen a poison or antidote like the reed?
Have you seen a more intimate companion and lover?

It sings of the path of blood;
it relates the passion of Majnun.
Only to the senseless is this sense confided.
Does the tongue have any patron but the ear?

Our days grow more unseasonable,
these days which mix with grief and pain . . .
but if the days that remain are few,
let them go; it doesn't matter. But You, You remain,
for nothing is as pure as You are.

All but the fish quickly have their fill of His water;
and the day is long without His daily bread.
The raw do not understand the state of the ripe,
so my words will be brief.

Break your bonds, be free, my child!
How long will silver and gold enslave you?
If you pour the whole sea into a jug,
will it hold more than one day's store?

The greedy eye, like the jug, is never filled.
Until content, the oyster holds no pearl.
Only one who has been undressed by Love
is free of defect and desire.

O Gladness, O Love, our partner in trade,
healer of all our ills, our Plato and Galen,
remedy of our pride and our vanity.

With love this earthly body could soar in the air;
the mountain could arise and nimbly dance.

Love gave life to Mount Sinai, O lover.
Sinai was drunk; Moses lost consciousness.

Pressed to the lips of one in harmony with myself,
I might also tell all that can be told;
but without a common tongue, I am dumb,
even if I have a hundred songs to sing.

When the rose is gone and the garden faded,
you will no longer hear the nightingale's song.
The Beloved is all; the lover just a veil.
The Beloved is living; the lover a dead thing.

If Love witholds its strengthening care,
the lover is left like a bird without wings.
How will I be awake and aware
if the light of the Beloved is absent?

Love wills that this Word be brought forth.
If you find the mirror of the heart dull,
the rust has not been cleared from its face.
O friends, listen to this tale,
the marrow of our inward state.

MATHNAWI I, 1–35
(*translated by Kabir Helminski*)

The Intellectual

The intellectual is always showing off;
the lover is always getting lost.
The intellectual runs away, afraid of drowning;
the whole business of love is to drown in the sea.
Intellectuals plan their repose;
lovers are ashamed to rest.
The lover is always alone, even surrounded with people;
like water and oil, he remains apart.
The man who goes to the trouble
of giving advice to a lover
gets nothing. He's mocked by passion.
Love is like musk. It attracts attention.
Love is a tree, and lovers are its shade.

FURUZANFAR #1957
(translated by Kabir Helminski)

In Restless Movement

If you don't see the hidden River,
see how the waterwheel of stars continually turns.
If the heavens receive no rest from being moved by Love,
heart, don't ask for rest—be a circling star.

Do you think God lets you cling to any branch?
Wherever you make an attachment, it will be broken.
Before God everything is like a ball,
subjected to and prostrating before the bat.
How should you, O my heart,
being only one of a hundred billion particles,
not be in restless movement at Love's command?

MATHNAWI VI, 913–915; 926–927
(*translated by Kabir Helminski and Camille Helminski*)

The Ship Sunk in Love

Should Love's heart rejoice unless I burn?
For my heart is Love's dwelling.
If You will burn Your house, burn it, Love!
Who will say, "It's not allowed"?
Burn this house thoroughly!
The lover's house improves with fire.
From now on I will make burning my aim,
for I am like the candle: burning only makes me brighter.
Abandon sleep tonight; traverse for one night
the region of the sleepless.

Look upon these lovers who have become distraught
and like moths have died in union with the One Beloved.
Look upon this ship of God's creatures
and see how it is sunk in Love.

MATHNAWI VI, 617–623
(translated by Kabir Helminski and Camille Helminski)

THE INTEREST WITHOUT THE CAPITAL

The lover's food is the love of the bread;
no bread need be at hand:
no one who is sincere in his love is a slave to existence.

Lovers have nothing to do with existence;
lovers have the interest without the capital.

Without wings they fly around the world;
without hands they carry the polo ball off the field.

That dervish who caught the scent of Reality
used to weave baskets even though his hand had been cut off.

Lovers have pitched their tents in nonexistence:
they are of one quality and one essence, as nonexistence is.

MATHNAWI III, 3020–3024
(translated by Kabir Helminski and Camille Helminski)

Your Bread Is Seeking You

Listen, put trust in God,
don't let your hands and feet tremble with fear:
your daily bread is more in love with you, than you with it.

It is in love with you and is holding back
only because it knows of your lack of self-denial.

If you had any self-denial, the daily bread
would throw itself upon you as lovers do.
What is this feverish trembling for fear of hunger?
With trust in God one can live full-fed.

MATHNAWI V, 2851–2854
(translated by Kabir Helminski and Camille Helminski)

Be Love's Willing Slave

Come and be Love's willing slave,
for Love's slavery will save you.
Forsake the slavery of this world
and take up Love's sweet service.
The free, the world enslaves,
but to slaves Love grants freedom.
I crave release from this world
like a bird from its egg;
free me from this shell that clings.
As from the grave, grant me new life.
O Love, O quail in the free fields of spring,
wildly sing songs of joy.

(translated by Camille Helminski with William Hastie)

GREED AND GENEROSITY

Look at her face.
Open your eyes into her eyes.
When she laughs, everyone falls in love.
Lift your head up off the table. See,
there are no edges to this garden.
Sweet fruits, every kind you can think of,
branches green and always
slightly moving.

How long should you look at earth's face?
Come back and look again.
Now you see the nervous greed
deep inside plants and animals. Now you see them
constantly giving themselves away.

Greed and generosity are evidence of love.
If you can't see love itself,
see the results.
If you can't find love-colors in anything,
look for the pale, tired face of a lover.
Take this town with its stores and everyone
rushing around, some with a lot of money,
some without any.

FURUZANFAR #1101
(translated by John Moyne and Coleman Barks)

After Being in Love,
the Next Responsibility

Turn me like a waterwheel turning a millstone.
Plenty of water, a Living River.
Keep me in one place and scatter the love.
Leaf-moves in wind, straw drawn toward amber,
all parts of the world are in love,
but they do not tell their secrets. Cows grazing
on a sacramental table, ants whispering in Solomon's ear.
Mountains mumbling an echo. Sky, calm.
If the sun were not in love, he would have no brightness,
the side of the hill no grass on it.
The ocean would come to rest somewhere.

Be a lover as they are, that you come to know
your Beloved. Be faithful that you may know
Faith. The other parts of the universe did not accept
the next responsibility of love as you can.
They were afraid they might make a mistake
with it, the inspired knowing
that springs from being in love.

FURUZANFAR #2674
(*translated by Coleman Barks*)

When Grapes Turn to Wine

When grapes turn
to wine, they long for our ability to change.

When stars wheel
around the North Pole,
they are longing for our growing consciousness.

Wine got drunk with us,
not the other way.
The body developed out of us, not we from it.

We are bees,
and our body is a honeycomb.
We made
the body, cell by cell we made it.

(translated by Robert Bly)

Ghazal

Oh no, an intellectual among *her* lovers!?
    a beauty like her? Faugh! Impossible!
Keep the brainy ones far from her door, keep the bathhouse
    dung smoke from the East Wind!
Sorry, no intellectuals admitted here. . . . but a lover? Ah, a
    hundred salaams!
Intellect deliberates, Intellect reflects—and meanwhile Love
    evaporates into the stratosphere.
By the time Intellect finds a camel for the Hajj, Love has
    climbed Mt. Sinai.
Love comes and gags me: "Scribbler! Forget mere verse. The
    starship departs!"

(translated by Peter Lamborn Wilson)

Intellect Is a Shackle

O my child, intellect is a shackle
on the foot of one who walks the Path.
Break the bond; the Way is open!
The intellect is a chain, the heart may be deceptive,
and even your soul is a veil—
the Path is hidden from all three.

When you lift the intellect, soul, and heart,
the station of nearness you reach is still subjective.
One who gets lost isn't considered brave.
Love takes aim at the one who has no troubles.
Know that the arrow of the Friend is ready in the bow.
Make your chest a target in front of it.

Love isn't the work of the tender and the gentle;
Love is the work of wrestlers.
The one who becomes a servant of lovers
is really a fortunate sovereign.
Don't ask anyone about Love; ask Love alone about Love.
Love is a cloud that scatters pearls.

Love doesn't need me to translate; it translates for itself.
If you journey to the seventh heaven, Love is a useful ladder.
Wherever a caravan journeys, Love is its *qiblah*.
May this universe not deceive you, waylaying you from Love,
for this universe comes from you.
Let's go! Close your mouth like mother of pearl.

Be silent, for this tongue of yours is the enemy of the soul.
O child, Shams of Tabriz has arrived; the soul is full of joy
for the time has come to join in union with his sun.

(translated by Refik Algan and Camille Helminski)

THE INTELLECT SAYS

The intellect says: "The six directions are limits: there is no
    way out."
Love says: "There is a way. I have traveled it thousands of
    times."
The intellect saw thousands of markets beyond that market.
Lovers who drink the dregs of the wine reel from bliss to bliss;
The dark-hearted men of reason
Burn inwardly with denial.
The intellect says: "Do not go forward, annihilation contains
    only thorns."
Love laughs back: "The thorns are in you."
Enough words! Silence!
Pull the thorn of existence out of the heart! Fast!
For when you do, you will see thousands of rose gardens in
    yourself.

(translated by Andrew Harvey)

Both

"The Beloved is so sweet, so sweet," they repeat;
I show them the scars where His polo stick thrashed me.
"The Beloved is terrible, a maniac," they wail;
I show them my eyes, melting in His tender passion.

(translated by Andrew Harvey)

The Lovers' Tailor's Shop

The Lovers' Tailor's Shop: tomorrow I'll go there wrapped in
    my long cloak, with a hundred yards of madness.
The Tailor snips you from Jones and stitches you to Smith,
pairing you with one, separating you from the other,
sews your heart to one of them for a lifetime—such silken
    thread! wonderful stitches! miraculous hand!
Then, when your heart is fixed, he rips out the seam,
snick! snick! With the scissors of *"Get ye down from it!"**
All this sewing together and tearing apart bewilders me,
my mind reels at the variegations of
affirmation and obliteration.
The heart is a dust-board, he the geometer of the heart:
what a marvel of figures, numbers, realities,
and names he inscribes!
When he multiplies you, like a number, by somebody else,
what a sum he manifests with his arithmetic!

---

* Qur'an 2:38. God's command to Adam and Eve.

You've seen multiplication—now study division:
how he parcels up one drop into an Ocean!
By the algebra of Fate he balances all equations:
Silence! for thought itself breaks down at such wonders.

(translated by Peter Lamborn Wilson)

REBAB AND NEY

O my Beauty, your love,
like amber, attracts the heart.
The heart has run to you,
and we, like lovers, run after it.

My soul eats so much sugar
in the Egypt of Love,
that sugar pours
from the reed of my wailing.

O stately bird of good fortune,
you who've landed by the throne of God,
from the shadow of your love,
every moment, like falcons
souls fly to that throne.

What a happy garden and meadow,
where roses and iris grow
watered by love,
and gazelles graze nearby.

The eye doesn't see itself.
But, because of your mirror,

all eyes are beholding themselves
in the mirror now.

O God's Sun of Shams of Tabriz,
with your noble, piercing *ney*,
tune the *rebab* of my soul.
For through that *rebab* of the soul
God's voice can be heard.

(translated by Nevit Ergin with Camille Helminski)

Because I Cannot Sleep

Because I cannot sleep
I make music at night.
I am troubled by the one
whose face has the color of spring flowers.
I have neither sleep, nor patience,
neither a good reputation, nor disgrace.

A thousand robes of wisdom are gone.
All my good manners have moved a thousand miles away.

The heart and the mind are left angry with each other.
The stars and the moon are envious of each other.
Because of this alienation the physical universe
is getting tighter and tighter.

The moon says, "How long will I remain
suspended without a sun?"
Without Love's jewel inside of me,
let the bazaar of my existence be destroyed stone by stone.

O Love, You who have been called by a thousand names,
You who know how to pour the wine
into the chalice of the body,
You who give culture to a thousand cultures,
You who are faceless but have a thousand faces,

O Love, You who shape the faces
of Turks, Frenchmen, and Zanzibaris,
give me a glass from Your bottle,
or a handful of bhang from Your branch.

Remove the cork once more.
Then we'll see a thousand chiefs prostrate themselves,
and a circle of ecstatic troubadours will play.
Then the addict will be freed of craving,
and will be resurrected,
and stand in awe till Judgment Day.

(translated by Kabir Helminski with Lail Fouladvend)

What Remains after Nothing

Love is the flame which, when it blazes,
consumes everything other than the Beloved.
The lover wields the sword of *Nothingness**
in order to dispatch all but God:
consider what remains after *Nothing*.
There remains *but God*: all the rest is gone.
Praise to you, O mighty Love, destroyer of all other "gods."

MATHNAWI V, 588–590
(translated by Kabir Helminski and Camille Helminski)

* The "la" of "*La illaha il Allah.*" (There are no gods but God.) Qur'an 3:62.

Love Is Reckless

Love is reckless; not reason.
Reason seeks a profit.
Love comes on strong, consuming herself, unabashed.

Yet, in the midst of suffering,
Love proceeds like a millstone,
hard-surfaced and straightforward.

Having died to self-interest,
she risks everything and asks for nothing.
Love gambles away every gift God bestows.

Without cause God gave us Being;
without cause, give it back again.
Gambling yourself away is beyond any religion.

Religion seeks grace and favor,
but those who gamble these away are God's favorites,
for they neither put God to the test
nor knock at the door of gain and loss.

MATHNAWI VI, 1967–1974
(translated by Kabir Helminski with Lail Fouladvend)

· 17 ·

Mercy

Now some men have so followed their highest intelligence that they have become totally angelic and pure light. These are prophets and saints who are free of fear and hope, *the persons on whom no fear shall come, and who shall not be grieved* [10:62]. There are others whose intellects have been so overcome by their lust that they have become totally bestial. Still others remain in the struggle. They are the group within whom a certain agony or anguish is manifested and who are not content with their lives. They are the faithful. The saints stand waiting to bring them to their own station and make them like themselves. The devils also lie in wait to pull them down to their level at the lowest depth.

When the assistance of God shall come, and the victory . . . [110:1]. The exoteric interpreters have interpreted this passage to mean that the Prophet's ambition was to make the world Muslim and to bring all men to God's way. . . .

The mystics, on the other hand, say that the meaning is as follows: a person imagines that he can rid himself of his base characteristics by means of his own action and endeavor. When he strives and expends much energy only to be disappointed, God says to him, "You thought it would come about through your own energy and action and deeds. That is indeed a custom I have established, that is, that what you have you should expend on Our behalf. Only then does Our mercy come. We say to you, 'Travel this endless road on your own weak legs.' We know that with your weak legs you will never be able to finish the way—in a hundred thousand years you would not finish even one stage of the way. Only when you make the effort and come onto the road to fall down at last, unable to go another step, only then will you be uplifted by God's favor. A child is picked up and carried while it is nursing, but when it grows older it is left to go on its own; so now when you have no strength left you are carried by God's favor. When you had the strength and could expend your energy, from time to time in a state between sleep and wakefulness, We bestowed upon you grace for you to gain strength in your quest and to encourage you. Now that you no longer have the means to continue, look upon Our grace and favor and see how they swarm down upon you. For a hundred thousand endeavors you would not have seen so much as an iota of this. *Now celebrate the praise of the Sustainer, and ask pardon of Him* [110:3]. Seek forgiveness for your thoughts and realize that you were only imagining that all this could come from your own efforts. You did not see that it all comes from Us. Now that you have seen that it is from Us, seek forgiveness." *He is inclined to forgive* [110:3].

FIHI MA FIHI #17

LOSING THE WAY

What wisdom was this, that the Object of all desire
caused me to leave my home joyously on a fool's errand,
so that I was actually rushing to lose the way
and at each moment being taken farther from what I sought—
and then God in His beneficence made that very wandering
the means of my reaching the right road and finding wealth!

He makes losing the way a way to true faith;
He makes going astray a field for the harvest of righteousness,
so that no righteous one may be without fear
and no traitor may be without hope.
The Gracious One has put the antidote in the poison
so that they may say He is the Lord of hidden grace.

MATHNAWI VI, 4339–4344
(translated by Kabir Helminski and Camille Helminski)

The Best Customer

If you want a customer who will pay in gold,
could there be a better customer than God, O my heart?
He buys our dirty bag of goods,
and in return gives us an inner light
lent from His splendor.
He receives the dissolving ice of this mortal body
and gives a kingdom beyond imagining.
He takes a few teardrops,
and gives a spiritual spring so delicious
sugar is jealous of its sweetness.
If any doubt waylays you,
rely upon the spiritual traders, the prophets.
The Divine Ruler increased their fortune so greatly,
no mountain could bear what they've been given.

MATHNAWI VI, 879–882; 886–887
(translated by Kabir Helminski)

Beggars Are Mirrors

Abundance is seeking the beggars and the poor,
just as beauty seeks a mirror.
Beggars, then, are the mirrors of God's bounty,
and they that are with God are united with
Absolute Abundance.

MATHNAWI I, 2745, 2750
(translated by Kabir Helminski and Camille Helminski)

The Embryo

You, who make demands within me like an embryo,
since You are the one who makes the demand,
make its fulfillment easy;
show the way, help me,
or else relinquish Your claim
and take this obligation from me!
Since You're demanding gold from a debtor,
Secretly give the gold, O rich King!

MATHNAWI III, 1490–1492
(*translated by Kabir Helminski and Camille Helminski*)

Muhammad and the Sick Companion

One of the companions fell ill
and became as thin as a thread.
The one who was entirely empathy and giving,
Muhammad, went to visit him.
Visiting the sick always brings benefits.
Maybe the sick person is a hidden saint,
or maybe he is a friend of the Way,
or he might at least have some relationship
to someone who is of the Way.
Even if he is your enemy,
your visit might turn him into a friend,
or at least lessen his dislike of you.
There is much more to be said,
but so as not to be tedious, the gist is this:

befriend the whole community.
Like a sculptor, if necessary,
carve a friend out of stone.
Realize that your inner sight is blind
and try to see a treasure in everyone.

When the Prophet arrived at the bedside,
the sick man was on his last breath.
When you are far from the saints,
in reality you are far from God.
Muhammad dealt so tenderly with his old friend
that the man came to life again.
"My sickness has been a blessing,
because it brought you here this morning!
I am happy with my fever,
with lying awake at night,
rather than sleeping all night like a buffalo,
and for the pain in my back
that woke me at midnight.
Pain is a treasure of mercy.
Behind its thick rind is a delicious fruit."

Be a fellow traveler with grief,
a companion of desolation,
find a long life in the dying of your self.
Don't listen to what your body craves.
Take your counsel elsewhere,
if you don't wish to end in regret.
Know that your *nafs*, your lower self, has womanly wiles,

and while a woman's wiles may be incomplete,
your *nafs* is totally beguiling.
If you ask your *nafs* what to do,
do the opposite of what she says.
For she can cause you to lose all discernment.
She will offer you the same promise
she has broken a thousand times.
If your life were lengthened a hundred years,
your *nafs* would offer new pretexts daily.
She utters cold and vain promises
as if they came from a warm heart.
This sorceress can bind the manhood of a man.
This little worm on the way can grow into a dragon.
The *nafs* is a sea of calm deception until it roars.
The *nafs* is a Hell that radiates little heat.
The *nafs* is an ankle-deep river you drown in.

The owner of a house knows when it was built,
while the spider in the corner has no idea.
The worm who has made his home in dry wood
has no idea of when the wood was fresh with sap.
And if a worm knew these origins,
it would be the essential substance of Intelligence
in the outward form of a worm.
Although your intelligence is ascending,
the bird of conditioning feeds on the ground.
Conditioning is the bane of our souls,
something borrowed we take as our own.
Better to be ignorant of worldly concerns,

better to be mad and to flee from self-interest,
better to drink poison and spill the water of life,
better to revile those who praise you,
and lend both the capital and the interest to the poor,
forgo safety and make a home in danger.
Sacrifice your reputation and become notorious.
I have tried caution and forethought;
from now on I will make myself mad.
The Prophet said to his suffering friend,
"Maybe it was something you prayed for,
or something you shouldn't have eaten.
Can you remember what sort of prayer you said
when you were being troubled by your *nafs*?"
"I can't remember," he said, "but perhaps
if you direct your spiritual influence to me,
it will come to mind." Then through
the light-giving presence of Muhammad
the light that separates truth from falsehood
flashed through the window between hearts.

"Now I remember, the foolish prayer I uttered.
I felt I was drowning in my negativity.
There was no hope of room for patience
and no means of escape,
no way to either repent or rebel
I felt I could not undo the lock.
Then in my prayer I asked to receive
the punishment I deserved in this life.
I would be happier to suffer the light pain of this world

than to suffer the pain of the other world.
It would be better to face the struggle now,
to put restraint upon myself now,
to lay upon myself the pain of serving God.
And so this sickness was laid upon me,
and I lost all power to continue my zikr.
I would surely have died if you had not revived me."

And then the merciful Prophet said,
"Hey! Don't pray like this ever again.
Don't dig yourself up by the roots."

The sick companion answered:
"This world is the Desert, and you are our Moses.
We remain in the desert because of our sin.
We are traveling for years and still we remain
in the first stage of our journey."

Pain will arise from looking within,
and the pain will remove the veil of self-conceit.
Until the mother faces the pain of childbirth,
the child cannot be born.
The Divine Trust is in the heart,
and the heart is pregnant:
the counsels of the prophets
and the wise are like the midwife.
Whoever is without pain is a robber,
because to be without pain is to say "I am God."
To say "I" at the wrong time is a curse;
at the right time it is a blessing.

We need to behead the rooster that crows too early.
What is the "beheading"?
Killing the *nafs* with spiritual work.
But nothing will overcome this *nafs*
except placing yourself under the shadow of the Pir,
and taking his sleeve. Even your grasping
is done through the help of God.
Know the truth of the words:
You did not throw when you threw. . . .
Whatever the soul sows is from the Soul of the soul.
He is the One who takes the hand,
and He is the One who carries the burden.
Hope to receive the breath of inspiration from that Source.

If you say that evil is from God, it is also true.
A painter can paint that which is beautiful
and that which is ugly with equal skill.
Both display his mastery. God is the creator
of those in denial as well as those who are faithful.

Finally the Prophet said to the sick man:
"Pray like this: O You who make easy what is hard,
give us good in this home and our future home.
Make our way to be a garden, for You are our goal."
At the Final Gathering the faithful will ask,
"O Angel, isn't Hell the common road
of faithful and deniers alike?
Yet we saw no smoke and fire on the road we traveled.
It seemed to us like paradise and a place of safety.

Where was the dangerous passage?"
And the Angel will say,
"The green gardens through which you passed,
that was Hell, but you saw it as lush and green.
Because you quenched the fires of your Hellish ego
for God's sake, your lust has turned to purity;
your greed has turned to unselfishness,
and the thorns of envy have become roses.
You turned your own fiery soul into an orchard
where the nightingales of remembrance could sing,
as if in a garden by the riverside.
Because you have brought water
into the blazing fire of your soul,
Hell has become a rose garden to you."

MATHNAWI I, 2140–2580
(translated by Kabir Helminski)

Why Be Cruel to Yourself

Your grace is the shepherd of all who have been created,
guarding them from the wolf of pain—
a loving shepherd like God's pen, Moses.
A single sheep fled from him: Moses wore out his shoes
and his feet blistered as he followed after it.
He continued searching until night fell;
meanwhile the flock had vanished from sight.
The lost sheep was weak and exhausted;
Moses shook the dust from it
and stroked its back and head with his hand,
fondling it lovingly like a mother.
Not a bit of irritation and anger,
nothing but love and pity and tears!
He said to the sheep, "I can understand
that you naturally had no pity on me,
but why did your nature show such cruelty to itself?"
At that moment God said to the angels,
"This human being is suitable to be a prophet."

MATHNAWI VI, 3280–3287
(translated by Kabir Helminski and Camille Helminski)

Generosity Is Gainful Trade

O sea of bliss, You have stored
transcendental forms of consciousness in the heedless,
You have stored a wakefulness in sleep,
You have fastened dominion over the heart
to the state of one who has lost her heart.

You conceal riches in the lowliness of poverty;
You fasten the necklace of wealth to poverty's iron collar.
Opposite is secretly concealed in opposite:
fire is hidden within boiling water.
A delightful garden is hidden within Nimrod's fire.

Income multiplies from giving and spending—
so that Muhammad, the king of prosperity, has said,
"O possessors of wealth, generosity is a gainful trade."
Riches were never lessened by sharing:
in truth, acts of charity increase one's wealth.

Mathnawi VI, 3567–3573
(*translated by Kabir Helminski*)

The Funny Thing Is . . .

When I want to leave
You hold my feet and won't let me go.
You steal my heart,
and sit on top of it.

Because of the secret You whispered,
and the moon You revealed,
Love's wind whirls in my head
and my heart loses its hands and feet.

You pass many nights in vigil,
and soar across this sky-dome with the wings of fasting,
in love with flight.

You saw me lost, waving and crying,
and said, "I am the guide.
I'll show you the road
for which you have been searching."

I'm hidden behind the wall,
and yet I'm right beside you.
You are oppressed and suffering,
yet I am near.

You who are anxious to get
where you think you're going,
I'll make your dreams come true.
I'll cook well every pot you try to boil.

My friend, you thought you lost Him;
that all your life you've been separated from Him.
Filled with wonder, you've always looked outside for Him,
and haven't searched within your own house.

The funny part is
that in this search,
Beauty has always accompanied you.
Wherever you have been,
He is the One holding your hand.

Keep looking for Him with Him;
You and He are on the same road.
O Beloved, You're so obvious
You're hidden from sight!

(translated by Camille Helminski and Kabir Helminski
with Nevit Ergin)

WHEN SAND SUFFICES

When you have no cleansing water,
sand suffices—
the Prophet gave this rule to those in need,
and still it continues.

Do you know why, O faithful ones?
Listen to the truth the wise reveal—
often in the desert, water is unseen,
but for the traveler sand abounds.

From the desert I will guide
the one who calls me guide

to the place where living waters flow,
to the Garden Love encompasses.

There, bathe in abundance,
drought dispelled,
for once you've washed in that stream,
the need for sand disappears;

Freed of any method,
purely by Spirit you'll be ruled.
O Master! Your exalted soul has seen
the Truth through every veil.

(translated by Camille Helminski with William Hastie)

O DROP

Listen, O drop, give yourself up without regret,
and in exchange gain the Ocean.
Listen, O drop, bestow upon yourself this honor,
and in the arms of the Sea be secure.
Who indeed should be so fortunate?
An Ocean wooing a drop!
In God's name, in God's name, sell and buy at once!
Give a drop, and take this Sea full of pearls.

MATHNAWI IV, 2619–2622
(translated by Kabir Helminski and Camille Helminski)

· 18 ·

Purity

I F YOU SPEAK WELL OF ANOTHER, the good will return to you.
The good and praise you speak of another you speak in reality
of yourself. A parallel would be when someone plants a garden
and herb bed around his house. Every time he looks out he sees
flowers and herbs. If you accustom yourself to speak well of
others, you are always in a "paradise." When you do a good deed
for someone else you become a friend to him, and whenever he
thinks of you he will think of you as a friend—and thinking of
a friend is as restful as a flower garden. When you speak ill of
someone else, you become detestable in his sight so that when-
ever he thinks of you he will imagine a snake or a scorpion, or
thorns and thistles. Now, if you can look at the flowers in a gar-
den day and night, why would you wander in a briar patch or a
snake pit? Love everybody so that you may always stay among
the flowers of the garden. If you hate everybody and imagine
enemies everywhere, it would be like wandering day and night
in a briar patch or snake pit.

The saints love everybody and see everything as good, not
for anyone else's sake but for their own, lest a hateful, detest-
able image come into their view. Since there is no choice in this
world but to think of people, the saints have striven to think

of everybody as a friend so that hatred may not mar their way.

So, everything you do with regard to people and every mention you make of them, good or evil, will all return to you. Hence God says, *"He who doth right, doth it to the advantage of his own soul; and he who doth evil, doth it against the same"* [41:46], and *"Whoever shall have wrought evil of the weight of an ant, shall behold the same"* [99:8].

FIHI MA FIHI #15

QUATRAINS FROM *OPEN SECRET*
(translated by John Moyne and Coleman Barks)

For years, copying other people, I tried to know myself.
From within, I couldn't decide what to do.
Unable to see, I heard my name being called.
Then I walked outside.

FURUZANFAR #77

✦ ✦ ✦

Take someone who doesn't keep score,
who's not looking to be richer, or afraid of losing,
who has not the slightest interest even
in his own personality: he's free.

FURUZANFAR #116

* * *

Stay in the company of lovers.
Those other kinds of people, they each
want to show you something.
A crow will lead you to an empty barn,
A parrot to sugar.

* * *

The sufi opens his hands to the universe
and gives away each instant, free.
Unlike someone who begs on the street for money to survive,
a dervish begs to give you his life.

FURUZANFAR #686

* * *

For a while we lived with people,
but we saw no sign in them of the faithfulness we wanted.
It's better to hide completely within
as water hides in metal, as fire hides in a rock.

FURUZANFAR #1082

* * *

Inside the Great Mystery that is,
we don't really own anything.
What is this competition we feel then,
before we go, one at a time, through the same gate?

FURUZANFAR #1616

No "Above" or "Below"

The really holy never need to be honored; their selves are already honored by Love. If a lamp wants to be placed where it can be seen, it wants that for others' sake, not its own. What does the lamp care whether it is placed "above" or "below"? Wherever it is, it is still a lamp, and it still gives out light. Nevertheless, it wants its light to reach and help others. Imagine if the sun were below the earth—it would still be the sun, of course, but the world would languish in darkness. So the sun is placed in its regal position not for its own sake at all, but for the world's. The real holy ones who are put in high positions are like the lamp and the sun—they do not care about "high" or "low," "above" or "below," and do not look to be revered by others.

Whenever Vision unfurls its ecstatic flag in you, or your mind blazes from a lightning flash of grace from heaven, you are, in that moment, cold to "above" and "below," to all status and rank, mastery or leadership, all man-made titles, praises, elevations, honors. None of these things concern you: you soar like a hawk in the cloudless sky of union.

If such splendor breaks over ordinary seekers, imagine how little the really holy ones, who are the mines themselves of that Love and that Splendor, could possibly care for "below" and "above"! No categories of any kind chain or even interest them; all their glorying is in God, and God is utterly free of anything we know as "above" or "below." "Above" and "below" belong to those of us who have heads and feet and deluded imaginations in the service of the tyrants of our false selves. Mohammed, may he always rest in peace, said once: "Do not make me out to be greater than Jonah, just because his ascension was in a whale's belly while mine took place in Heaven and on the Throne." What the Prophet meant was this: "For God, the whale's belly is the same as the Throne."

(translated by Andrew Harvey)

A THIEF IN THE NIGHT

Suddenly
 (yet somehow expected)
he arrived
 the guest ...
the heart trembling
 "Who's there?"
 and soul responding
  "The Moon ..."

came into the house
 and we lunatics
ran into the street
 stared up
  looking
   for the moon.

Then—inside the house—
 he cried out
"Here I am!"
 and we
beyond earshot
 running around
  calling him ...

crying for him
    for the drunken nightingale
locked lamenting
    in our garden
while we
    mourning ring doves
        murmured "Where
            where?"

As if at midnight
    the sleepers bolt upright
in their beds
    hearing a thief
break into the house
    in the darkness
they stumble about
    crying "Help!
        A thief! A thief!"
but the burglar himself
    mingles in the confusion
echoing their cries:
    " . . . a thief!"
        till one cry
        melts with the others.

*And He is with you**
    with you

* Qur'an 4:57.

in your search
      when you seek Him
look for Him
      in your looking
closer to you
      than yourself
            to yourself:
Why run outside?
      Melt like snow.
wash yourself
      with yourself:
urged by Love
      tongues sprout
from the soul
      like stamens
      from the lily . . .
But learn
      this custom
from the flower:
      silence
            your tongue.

DIWAN–E SHAMS, v. V, ED. FURUZANFAR, # 2172
(translated by Peter Lamborn Wilson)

Emptiness

Does anyone write something on a place
that has already been written over,
or plant a sapling where one already grows?
No; he seeks a blank piece of paper
and sows the seed where none has yet been sown.
Sister, be bare earth;
be a clean piece of paper untouched by writing,
that you may be ennobled by *the pen of revelation,**
so that the Gracious One may sow seed within you.

MATHNAWI V, 1961–1964
(translated by Kabir Helminski and Camille Helminski)

The Empty Heart

Water in the boat is the ruin of the boat,
but water under the boat is its support.
Since Solomon cast the desire for wealth out from his heart,
he didn't call himself by any name but "poor."
The stoppered jar, though in rough water,
floated because of its empty heart.
When the wind of poverty is in anyone,
she floats in peace on the waters of this world.

MATHNAWI I, 985–988
(translated by Kabir Helminski and Camille Helminski)

* Qur'an 68:1, Surah Al-Qalam (The Pen), *Nun wa 'l Qalam* (opening words of this Surah).

The Guest House

Darling, the body is a guest house;
every morning someone new arrives.
Don't say, "O, another weight around my neck!"
or your guest will fly back to nothingness.
Whatever enters your heart is a guest
from the invisible world: entertain it well.

Every day, and every moment, a thought comes
like an honored guest into your heart.
My soul, regard each thought as a person,
for every person's value is in the thought they hold.

If a sorrowful thought stands in the way,
it is also preparing the way for joy.
It furiously sweeps your house clean,
in order that some new joy may appear from the Source.
It scatters the withered leaves from the bough of the heart,
in order that fresh green leaves might grow.
It uproots the old joy so that
a new joy may enter from Beyond.

Sorrow pulls up the rotten root
that was veiled from sight.
Whatever sorrow takes away or causes the heart to shed,
it puts something better in its place—
especially for one who is certain
that sorrow is the servant of the intuitive.

Without the frown of clouds and lightning,
the vines would be burned by the smiling sun.
Both good and bad luck become guests in your heart:
like planets traveling from sign to sign.
When something transits your sign, adapt yourself,
and be as harmonious as its ruling sign,
so that when it rejoins the Moon,
it will speak kindly to the Lord of the heart.

Whenever sorrow comes again,
meet it with smiles and laughter,
saying, "O my Creator, save me from its harm,
and do not deprive me of its good.
Lord, remind me to be thankful,
let me feel no regret if its benefit passes away."

And if the pearl is not in sorrow's hand,
let it go and still be pleased.
Increase your sweet practice.
Your practice will benefit you at another time;
someday your need will be suddenly fulfilled.

MATHNAWI V, 3644–3646; 3676–3688;
3693–3696; 3700–3701
(translated by Kabir Helminski)

EXPANSION AND CONTRACTION

Before everything you own slips away
tell the material world, like Mary:
My refuge is with the Merciful.

In her room Mary had seen something
that won her heart, something intensely alive.
That trusted spirit rose from the face of the earth
like a sun or moon rising in the East,
like beauty unveiled.

Mary, who was undressed, began to tremble,
afraid of the evil that might be in it.
This kind of thing could cause
Joseph to cut his own wrist.
It flowered in front of her like a rose,
like a fantasy that lifts its head in the heart.

Mary became selfless and in this selflessness
she said, "I will leap into God's protection,"
because that pure-bosomed one
could take herself to the Unseen.
Since she thought this world a temporary kingdom,
she built her fortress in Presence,
so that in the hour of death
she would be invulnerable.

She saw no better protection than God;
she made her home near to His castle.
Those glances of love were arrows,
piercing and killing all reason.
The army and its leaders are enthralled by Him.
Those with wit are made witless by Him.
Hundreds of thousands of kings are in His service.
Hundreds of thousands of full moons
are dedicated to the all-night fever of His love.
Zuhra cannot breathe a word;
universal reason, on seeing Him, is humbled.

What shall I say? He has sealed my lips.
The channel of my breath is hooked up to His furnace.
"I am the smoke of that fire, the evidence of it."
The only evidence for the sun is its towering light.
What shadow could claim itself to be that evidence?
It is enough for the shadow to submit itself before Him.
The majesty of this evidence declares the truth.

He is ahead, and all perceptions must fall behind.
All perceptions are riding on lame donkeys,
while He is riding on an arrow traveling through space.
If He chooses to escape,
none can even find the dust He leaves behind;
and if they choose to flee, He simply bars the way.

Every perception is disquieting:
this is the moment for struggle, not for lifting the goblet.
One bird of perception is soaring like a falcon,
another is tearing through the air like an arrow,
another is out sailing like a ship,
and another is constantly turning back.

When something to chase appears in the distance,
all these birds speed toward it,
but when it disappears, they are lost.
Like owls they return to the wilderness,
waiting, with one eye open and one eye closed,
for some prey to appear.
If they have to wait too long, they wonder,
was it something real or not?

The best course would be to rest a while
and gather some strength and vigor.
If night never came, people would waste themselves
pursuing all that they desire.
They would give their own bodies to be consumed
for the sake of their desire and greed,
but night appears, a treasure of Mercy,
to save them from desires for a short while.
When you feel contraction, traveler,
it's for your own good. Don't burn with grief.

In the state of expansion and delight
you are spending something, and that spending
needs the income of pain.

If it were always summertime,
the blazing heat would burn the garden,
soil and roots, so that nothing would ever grow again.
December is grim yet kind;
summer is all laughter, and yet it burns.
When contraction comes, see the expansion in it;
be cheerful, don't frown.
The children laugh; the sages look serious.
Sorrow is from the liver and laughter from the lungs.
The eyes of a child, like those of an ass,
are fixed only on its stall;
while the eyes of the wise see to the end.

MATHNAWI III, 3700–3741
(*translated by Kabir Helminski*)

THE GOOD ROOT

Are you fleeing from Love because of a single humiliation?
What do you know of Love except the name?
Love has a hundred forms of pride and disdain,
and is gained by a hundred means of persuasion.
Since Love is loyal, it purchases one who is loyal:
it has no interest in a disloyal companion.
The human being resembles a tree;

your root is a covenant with God:
that root must be cherished with all one's might.
A feeble covenant is a rotten root, without grace or fruit.
Though the boughs and leaves of the date palm are green,
greenness brings no benefit if the root is corrupt.
If a branch is without green leaves, yet has a good root,
a hundred leaves will put forth their hands in the end.

MATHNAWI V, 1163–1169
(translated by Kabir Helminski and Camille Helminski)

✦ ✦ ✦

Abandon the dry prayer of words,
for the tree presupposes the scattering of seeds.
Yet even if you have no seed, due to your prayer,
God will bestow upon you a palm tree
saying, "How well did he labor!"
Like Mary—she had heartfelt pain, but no seed:
an artful One made that withered palm tree green for her sake.
Because that noble lady was loyal to God,
God fulfilled a hundred desires without desire on her part.

MATHNAWI V, 1188–1191
(translated by Kabir Helminski and Camille Helminski)

When a Man and a Woman Become One

I darkened my eyes
with the dust of sadness
until each of them was a sea full of pearls.

All the tears which we creatures shed for Him
are not tears as many think but pearls. . . .

I am complaining about the Soul of the soul,
but I'm no complainer; I'm simply saying how it is.

My heart tells me it is distressed with Him,
but I can only laugh at such pretended injuries.

Be fair, You who are the Glory of the just.
You, Soul, free of "we" and "I,"
subtle spirit within each man and woman.

When a man and a woman become one,
that "one" is You.
And when that one is obliterated, there You are.

Where is this "we" and this "I"?
By the side of the Beloved.
You made this "we" and this "I"
in order that you might play
this game of courtship with Yourself,
that all "you's" and "I's" might become one soul
and finally drown in the Beloved.

All this is true. Come!
You who are the Creative Word: Be.
You, so far beyond description.

Is it possible for the bodily eye to see You?
Can thought comprehend Your laughter or grief?
Tell me now, can it possibly see You at all?
Such a heart has only borrowed things to live with.

The garden of love is green without limit
and yields many fruits other than sorrow or joy.
Love is beyond either condition:
without spring, without autumn, it is always fresh.

MATHNAWI I, 1779–1794
(*translated by Kabir Helminski*)

SIFTER OF DUST

Suppose you know the definitions
of all substances and their products,
what good is this to you?
Know the true definition of yourself.
That is essential.
Then, when you know your own definition, flee from it,
that you may attain to the One who cannot be defined,
O sifter of the dust.

MATHNAWI V, 564–565
(*translated by Kabir Helminski and Camille Helminski*)

The House of Love

Why is there always music in this house?
Ask the owner.

Idols inside the Kaaba?
God's light in a pagan temple?

Here is a treasure this world could not contain.
The house and its landlord
are all pretext and play.

Hands off this house, this talisman.
Don't argue with the landlord;
he's drunk every night.

The dirt and garbage are musk and rose.
The roof and door are music and verse.
In short, whoever finds this house
is ruler of the world, Solomon of his time.

Look down, Lord, from the roof;
bless us with your glance.

I swear, since seeing Your face,
the whole world is a fraud and fantasy.
The garden is bewildered as to what is leaf
or blossom. The distracted birds
can't distinguish the birdseed from the snare.

A house of love with no limits,
a presence more beautiful than Venus or the moon,
a beauty whose image fills the mirror of the heart.

Zulaikha's female friends,
beside themselves in Joseph's presence, sliced their wrists.
Maybe a curl of his hair brushed their hearts.

Come in. The Beloved is here. We are all drunk.
No one notices who enters or leaves.
Don't sit outside the door in the dark, wondering.

Those drunk with God,
even if they are a thousand, live as One.
But drunk with lust, even one is double.

Enter the thicket of lions unafraid of any wounds.
The shadows you fear are just a child's fantasy.

There is no wound and nothing to be wounded;
all is mercy and love.
But you build up thought
like a massive wooden door.
Set fire to the wood.
Silence the noise of the heart.
Hold your harmful tongue.

(translated by Kabir Helminski)

Who Are You and
What Do You Want?

He said, "Who is at the door?"
I said, "Your humble slave."
He said, "Why have you come?"
I said, "To offer salaams."
He said, "How long will you wait?"
I said, "Until you call."
He said, "How long will you boil?"
I said, "Until you resurrect me."

I laid claim to love, swore oaths of love,
and told how I lost all power and position for love.
He said, "The judge asks to see your witness."
"These tears, these pale cheeks."
"Your witness has bloodshot eyes and cannot be trusted."
I said, "By your high justice, they are just and true."
He said, "Who was your companion?"
"Your gift of imaginal vision."
"What called you here?"
"The fragrance of your cup."

"What do you want?"
"Faithfulness and intimacy."
"What do you want from me?" He said.
"Your subtle grace," I said.
"Where is the greatest pleasure?"
"In Caesar's palace," I said.
"And what did you see there?"

"A hundred fascinations."

He said, "Then why is it so desolate?"

"For fear of thieves."

"Who is the thief?" He said.

"Whatever challenges our vanity,"* I said.

"Where is safety?" He said.

"In abstinence† and pure consciousness of God."‡

"What is abstinence?"

I said, "The way of peace."

"Where is catastrophe?"

"In the street of Your love."

"How do you travel there?" He asked.

"With integrity," I said.

Silence. If I were to utter more,

you would be completely gone.

left without a door or roof.

DIVAN, FURUZANFAR #436
(translated by Kabir Helminski)

---

* *Melamet.*
† *zuhd.*
‡ *taqwa*: fearing nothing but God.

Love Ends All Arguments

Dear soul, Love alone cuts arguments short,
for it alone comes to the rescue
when you cry for help against disputes.
Eloquence is dumbfounded by Love: it dares not wrangle,
for the lover fears that, if he answers back,
the pearl of inner experience might fall out of his mouth.

MATHNAWI V, 3240–3241
(*translated by Kabir Helminski and Camille Helminski*)

Bibliography

RUMI TRANSLATIONS AND PARAPHRASES

Arberry, A. J. *The Rubaiyat of Jalal al-Din Rumi (Translations from the Divan-i Shams-i Tabriz-i)*. London: E. Walker, 1949.

_____. *Mystical Poems of Rumi 1: First Selection, Poems 1–200*. Chicago: University of Chicago Press, 1968.

_____. *Discourses of Rumi (Fihi ma Fihi)*. London: J. Murray, 1975.

_____. *Mystical Poems of Rumi 2: Second Selection, Poems 201–400*. Chicago: University of Chicago Press, 1991.

Barks, Coleman. *Delicious Laughter*. Athens, Ga.: Maypop, 1990.

_____. *Like This*. Athens, Ga.: Maypop, 1990.

_____. *Feeling the Shoulder of the Lion*. Putney, Vt.: Threshold Books, 1991.

_____. *One-Handed Basket Weaving*. Athens, Ga.: Maypop, 1991.

_____. *Birdsong*. Athens, Ga.: Maypop, 1993.

_____. *The Essential Rumi*. San Francisco: Harper, 1995.

Barks, Coleman, and Robert Bly. *Night and Sleep*. Cambridge, Mass.: Yellow Moon Press, 1981.

Barks, Coleman, and John Moyne. *Open Secret*. Putney, Vt.:
Threshold Books, 1984.

_____. *Quatrains from Divan-i Shams-i Tabrizi*. Putney, Vt.:
Threshold Books, 1986.

_____. *We Are Three*. Athens, Ga.: Maypop, 1987.

_____. *These Branching Moments*. Providence, R.I.: Copper
Beech Press, 1988.

_____. *This Longing*. Putney, Vt.: Threshold Books, 1988.

Bly, Robert. *When Grapes Turn to Wine*. Cambridge, Mass.:
Yellow Moon Press, 1986.

Cave, George. *Sufi Poetry*. Rawalpindi, Pakistan: R.C.D.
Cultural Association, 1972.

Chittick, William. *The Sufi Path of Love: The Spiritual
Teachings of Rumi*. Albany, N.Y.: State University of New
York Press, 1983.

Cowan, James. *Where Two Oceans Meet: A Selection of Odes
from the Divan of Shems of Tabriz*. Rockport, Mass.:
Element, 1992.

Ergin, Nevit Oguz. *Crazy as We Are: Selected Rubais from
Divan-i Kebir*. Prescott, Ariz.: Hohn Press, 1992.

_____. *Magnificent One: Selected New Verses from Divan-i
Kebir*. Burdett, N.Y.: Larson Publications, 1993.

_____. *Divan-i Kebir, Meter 1–5*. Walla Walla, Wash.:
Current, 1995.

_____. *Divan-i Kebir, Meter 2*. Walla Walla, Wash.: Current, 1996.

Gupta, M. G. *Maulana Rumi's Masnavi (Mathnawi Rumi,
Verses 1–4563)*. Agra, India: MG Publishers, 1990.

Harvey, Andrew. *Love's Fire: Recreations of Rumi*. Ithaca, N.Y.: Meeramma, 1988.

———. *Speaking Flame*. Ithaca, N.Y.: Meeramma, 1989.

———. *The Way of Passion: A Celebration of Rumi*. Berkeley, Calif.: Frog, Ltd., 1994.

———. *Light upon Light: Inspirations from Rumi*. Berkeley, Calif.: North Atlantic Books, 1996.

———. *Love's Glory: Re-creations of Rumi*. Berkeley, Calif.: North Atlantic Books, 1996.

Hasan, Masudul. *Stories from Rumi*. Karachi, Pakistan: Ferozsons, 1977.

Hastie, William. *The Festival of Spring, from the Divan of Jelaluddin*. Edinburgh: McLehose, 1903.

Helminski, Camille, and Kabir Edmund Helminski. *Rumi—Daylight: A Daybook of Spiritual Guidance*. Putney, Vt.: Threshold Books, 1990.

———. *Jewels of Remembrance: A Daybook of Spiritual Guidance*. Brattleboro, Vt.: Threshold Books, 1996.

Helminski, Kabir Edmund. *The Ruins of the Heart: Selected Lyric Poetry of Jelaluddin Rumi*. Putney, Vt.: Threshold Books, 1981.

———. *Love Is a Stranger: Selected Lyric Poetry of Jelaluddin Rumi*. Putney, Vt.: Threshold Books, 1993.

Khalili, Nader. *Fountain of Fire*. Los Angeles: Burning Gate, 1996.

Khosla, Krishna Kumar. *The Sufism of Rumi*. Shaftesbury, Dorset: Element, 1987.

_____. *Rumi Speaks through Sufi Tales*. Chicago: Kazi
    Publications, 1996.
Liebert, Daniel. *Rumi—Fragments, Ecstasies*. Santa Fe, N.M.:
    Source Books, 1981.
Nicholson, R. A. *Tales of Mystic Meaning, Being Selections from
    the Mathnawi of Jalalud-Din Rumi*. London: Chapman
    and Hall, 1931.
_____. *The Mathnawi of Jalalu'ddin Rumi: Commentary*.
    London: Luzac, 1937–1940.
_____. *Rumi, Poet and Mystic, 1207–1273*. London: Allen
    and Unwin, 1956.
_____. *The Mathnawi of Jalalu'ddin Rumi*. London: Luzac, 1977.
Redhouse, James W. *Mesnevi of Mevlana (our Lord) Jelalu'd-
    Din, Muhammed, er-Rumi*. London: Trubner & Co., 1881.
Robinson, Samuel. *Persian Poetry for English Readers*.
    Glasgow: Printed for private circulation, 1883.
Schimmel, Annemarie. *Look! This Is Love: Poems of Rumi*.
    Boston, Mass.: Shambhala Publications, 1991.
Shiva, Shahram. *Rending the Veil: Literal and Poetic
    Translations of Rumi*. Prescott, Ariz.: Hohn Press, 1995.
Star, Jonathan, and Shahram Shiva. *A Garden Beyond
    Paradise: The Mystical Poetry of Rumi*. New York: Bantam
    Books, 1992.
Thackston, Wheeler M. *Signs of the Unseen: The Discourses
    of Jelaluddin Rumi (Fihi ma Fihi)*. Putney, Vt.: Threshold
    Books, 1994.
Wilson, C. E. *The Masnavi*. Karachi, Pakistan: Indus
    Publications, 1976.

Winfield, E. H. *Masnavi I Masnavi, the Spiritual Couplets of Maulana Jalalu-d'in Muhamad I Rumi*. London: Trubner & Co., 1887.

ANTHOLOGIES CONTAINING RUMI'S WRITINGS

Angha, Nahid. *Selections: Poems from Khayam, Rumi, Hafez, Moulana Shah Maghsoud*. San Rafael, Calif.: International Association of Sufism Publication, 1991.

Arberry, A. J. (ed.). *Persian Poems: An Anthology of Verse Translations*. New York: Dutton, 1964.

_____. *Immortal Rose: An Anthology of Persian Lyrics*. London: Luzac, 1983.

_____. *In Praise of Rumi*. Prescott, Ariz.: Hohm Press, 1989.

Barks, Coleman. *The Hand of Poetry: Five Mystic Poets of Persia*. New Lebanon, N.Y.: Omega Publications, 1993.

Browne, Edward Granville. *Edward G. Browne (Poems from the Persian)*. London: E. Benn, 1927.

Costello, Louisa Stuart (comp. and trans.). *The Rose Garden of Persia*. London: Longman, Brown, Green, and Longmans, 1900.

Davis, F. Hadland. *The Persian Mystics: Jalalud-Din Rumi*. New York: Dutton, 1908.

Dole, Nathan Haskell. *Flowers from Persian Poets*. New York: Thomas Y. Crowell, 1901.

Halpern, Daniel. *Holy Fire: Nine Visionary Poets and the Quest for Enlightenment*. New York: HarperPerennial, 1994.

Hasan, Hadi (ed.). *A Golden Treasury of Persian Poetry*. New Delhi, India: Indian Council for Cultural Relations, 1972.

Holden, Edward Singleton. *Flowers from Persian Gardens: Selections from the Poems of Saadi, Hafiz, Omar Khayyam, and Others*. New York: R. H. Russell, 1902.

Jackson, A. V. Williams. *Early Persian Poetry: From the Beginnings Down to the Time of Firdausi*. Boston, Mass.: Longwood Press, 1979

Nicholson, R. A. *Translations of Eastern Poetry and Prose*. London: Curzon, 1987.

Palmer, Edward Henry. *The Song of the Reed and Other Pieces*. London: Trubner & Co., 1877.

_____. *The Persian Poets*. New York: Crowell, 1901.

Pocock, Ebenezer. *Flowers of the East*. London: Hamilton, Adams, & Co., 1833.

_____. *The Shadow of the Bird in Flight*. New Delhi, India: Rupa & Co., 1994.

Pound, Omar. *Arabic and Persian Poems*. Washington, D.C.: Three Continents Press, 1986.

Wilson, Peter Lamborn. *The Drunken Universe: An Anthology of Persian Sufi Poetry*. Grand Rapids, Mich.: Phanes Press, 1987.

_____. *Sacred Drift: Essays on the Margins of Islam*. San Francisco: City Lights Books, 1993.

BOOKS ABOUT RUMI'S LIFE AND WORK

Aflaki, Shams al-Din Ahmad. *Legends of the Sufi: Selected Anecdotes from the Work Entitled The Acts of the Adepts (Menaqiba 'I arifln)*. London: Theosophical Publishing House, 1976.

_____. *The Hundred Tales of Wisdom: Life, Teachings, and Miracles of Jalaludin Rumi from Aflaki's Munaqib, Together with Certain Important Stories from Rumi's Works Traditionally Known as The Hundred Tales of Wisdom.* London: Octagon Press, 1978.

Ali, Mohamed. *The Life and Thought of Mohammad Jalaluddin Rumi.* Lahore, Pakistan: Bazm-i-Iqbal, n.d.

Arasteh, A. Reza. *Rumi, the Persian: Rebirth in Creativity and Love.* Lahore, Pakistan: Sh. Muhammad Ashraf, 1965.

_____. *Rumi the Persian, the Sufi.* London: Routledge & K. Paul, 1974.

Bayat, Mojdeh. *Tales from the Land of the Sufis.* Boston, Mass.: Shambhala Publications, 1994.

Chittick, William C. *The Sufi Doctrine of Rumi: An Introduction.* Tehran, Iran: Aryamehr University, 1974.

DeLamotte, Roy C. *Jalaluddin Rumi, Songbird of Sufism.* Lanham, Md.: University Press of America, 1980.

Friedlander, Shems. *The Whirling Dervishes: Being an Account of the Sufi Order Known as the Mevlevis and Its Founder the Poet and Mystic Mevlana Jalaluddin Rumi.* Albany, N.Y.: State University of New York Press, 1992.

Guvenc, R. Oruc. *Lovers of God, Mevlana.* Vaduz, Liechtenstein: Aconcagua, 1986.

Hakim, Khalifa Abdul. *The Metaphysics of Rumi, a Critical and Historical Sketch.* Lahore, Pakistan: Institute of Islamic Culture, 1959.

Hatman, Talat Sait. *Mevlana Celaleddin Rumi and the Whirling Dervishes: Sufi Philosophy, Whirling Rituals, Poems of Ecstasy, Miniature Paintings.* Istanbul: Dost Yayinlari, 1983.

Iqbal, Afzal. *The Life and Thought of Mohammad Jalal-ud-Din Rumi.* Lahore, Pakistan: Bazm-i-Iqbal, 1955.

_____. *Iqbal as a Thinker.* Lahore, Pakistan: Sh. Muhammad Ashraf, 1966.

Irfani, Khawaja Abdul Hamid. *The Sayings of Rumi and Iqbal.* Lahore, Pakistan: Research Society of Pakistan, University of the Punjab, 1986.

Lee, Kaela. *The Mouse and the Camel: A Fable Based on the Teaching Tale by Jalalu'l-Din Rumi.* Master's thesis, Bank Street College of Education (New York), 1994.

Lewisohn, Leonard (ed.). *Classical Persian Sufism from Its Origins to Rumi.* London: Khaniqahi Nimatullahi Publications, 1996.

McNaughton, Duncan. *Rumi Is Buried at Konya.* Bolinas, Calif.: D. McNaughton, 1973.

_____. *Mystics of the Book: Themes, Topics, and Typologies.* New York: P. Lang, 1993.

Nasr, Seyyed Hossein. *Jalal al-Din Rumi: Supreme Persian Poet and Sage.* Tehran, Iran: Conseil Superieur de la Culture et des Arts, 1974.

_____. *Rumi and the Sufi Tradition.* Tehran, Iran: RCD Cultural Institute, 1974.

New York University Near Eastern Round Table. *The Scholar and the Saint: Studies in Commemoration of Abul-Rayhan al-Biruni and Jalal al-Din al-Rumi.* New York: Hagop

Kevorkian Center for Near Eastern Studies, New York
University Press, 1975.

Onder, Mehmet. *Mevlana Jelaleddin Rumi*. Ankara, Turkey:
Culture Ministry, 1990.

_____. *Konya: The Residence of Great Mevlana, the Moslem
Mystic, and a Guide for the Ancient Art and Museums in
the City*. Istanbul: Keskin Colour Ltd. Co., 1970.

Paul, Harendrachandra. *Jalalud-Din Rumi and His Tasawwuf.*
Calcutta, India: Sobharani Paul, 1985.

_____. *Poetry and Mysticism in Islam: The Heritage of Rumi.*
New York: Cambridge University Press, 1994.

Qaiser, Nazir. *Rumi's Impact on Iqbal's Religious Thought*. La-
hore, Pakistan: Iqbal Academy Pakistan, 1989.

Renard, John. *All the King's Falcons: Rumi on Prophets and
Revelation*. Albany, N.Y.: State University of New York
Press, 1994.

Schimmel, Annemarie. *From Sanai to Maulana and Iqbal.*
Kabul, Afghanistan: University of Kabul, 1977.

_____. *I Am Wind, You Are Fire: The Life and Work of Rumi.*
Boston, Mass.: Shambhala Publications, 1992.

_____. *The Triumphal Sun: A Study of the Works of Jalaloddin
Rumi*. Albany, N.Y.: State University of New York Press,
1993.

Turkmen, Erkan. *Rumi as a True Lover of God; and, On the
First Eighteen Verses of Rumi's Masnevi*. Konya, Turkey:
Buyuk Anadolu Dersanesi, 1987.

_____. *Rumi as a True Lover of God: A Collection of Erkan*

Turkmen's Articles on Rumi. Istanbul: Baltac Tourism,
1990.

_____. *The Essence of Rumi's Masnevi.* Konya, Turkey: Mis-
ket, 1992.

Vitray-Meyerovitch, Eva de. *The Whirling Dervishes: A Com-
memoration.* London: International Rumi Committee,
1974.

_____. *Rumi and Sufism.* Sausalito, Calif.: Post-Apollo Press,
1987.

Credits

The editor wishes to thank the following authors for their kind permission to include their work in this collection:

John Moyne and Coleman Barks from various volumes originally published by Threshold Books.

Robert Bly from *Night and Sleep* and *When Grapes turn to Wine*, used by permission of the author.

Daniel Liebert from *Fragments, Ecstasies*, by permission of the author and of Source Books, Cedar Hill, Missouri.

Andrew Harvey from *Light Upon Light: Inspirations from Rumi*, copyright 1996, used by arrangement with North Atlantic Books, Berkeley, California.

Peter Lamborn Wilson from *Sacred Drift: Essays on the Margins of Islam*, appearing courtesy of City Lights Books, San Francisico, and based on rough translations by Dr. W. C. Chittick, and from *The Drunken Universe: An Anthology of Persian Sufi Poetry*, versions by Nasrollah Pourjavady and P. L. Wilson, courtesy of Phanes Press, Grand Rapids, Michigan.

Kabir Helminski and Camille Helminski for work never before published, as well as material that has been reworked from their earlier published versions.

We also wish to acknowledge various collaborators, including Refik Algan, Nevit Ergin, Lail Fouladvant, Alan Godlas,

Lida Saedian, and the late William Hastie, as well as other translators whose valuable work we have not been able to include in this volume.

Index of Titles and First Lines

Night cancels the business of the day, 87
No "Above" or "Below", 198
Nothing occupies us, Sir, 29

O brother, Wisdom is pouring into you, 137
O Drop, 194
O moon-faced Beloved, 56
O my Beauty, your love, 174
O my child, intellect is a shackle, 171
O my Sustainer, 155
O sea of bliss, You have stored, 191
O tongue, you are an endless treasure, 18
Oh no, an intellectual among *her* lovers, 170
On His Sepulchre, 28
On Resurrection Day God will ask, 35
One breath from the breath of the Lover, 107
One of the companions fell ill, 183
One, One, One, 121
One-Way Pull, The, 155
Only Certain Refuge, The, 150
Only Teaching, The, 31
Only the Heart, 83
Open Secret (quatrains), 196
Our fasting is over . . ., 104
Out of Control, 153
Owner of All States, The, 58

People are distracted by objects of desire, 16
Praising Manners, 9, 106
Precious Core, 90
Proper Vocation, 29